MY MASTER

General Sam Houston as the anti-secession Governor of Texas 1860-61.

Jeff Hamilton circa 1935 in Belton, Texas. *Photo courtesy of The Center for American History of the University of Texas at Austin.*

MY MASTER

The Inside Story of
Sam Houston
and His Times

By His Former Slave
JEFF HAMILTON

as told to
LENOIR HUNT

foreword by
FRANKLIN WILLIAMS

State✦House
Press
McMurry University
Abilene, Texas

Library of Congress Cataloging-in-Publication Data

Hamilton, Jeff, b. 1840
"My master": the inside story of Sam Houston and his times / by Jeff Hamilton as told to
Lenoir Hunt; with a foreword by Franklin Williams.
p. cm.
Originally published: Dallas, Tex.: Manfred, Van Nort & Co., c1940.
Includes bibliographical references and index.
ISBN 0-938349-84-8 (hardcover: acid-free paper)
ISBN 0-938349-86-4 (paper: acid-free paper)
ISBN 0-938349-85-6 (limited: acid-free paper)
ISBN-13: 978-1-933337-23-4 (paper PTO)
ISBN-10: 1-933337-23-0 (paper PTO)
1. Houston, Sam, 1793-1863--Friends and associates. 2. Hamilton, Jeff, b. 1840.
I. Hunt, Lenoir. II. Title.
F390.H84H35 1992
976.4'H84H35--dc20
92-4923
Revised

Printed in the United States of America

Cover Design by Rosenbohm Graphic Design
Cover Illustration:
Jeff Hamilton in 1934.
Etching by Bernhardt Wall from a photograph by Temple Houston Morrow.
Courtesy of The Center for American History of the University of Texas at Austin.

State House Press
McMurry Station, Box 637
Abilene, TX 79697-0637
(325) 572-3974
www.mcwhiney.org/press

Distributed by Texas A&M University Press Consortium
www.tamu.edu/upress • 1-800-826-8911

ISBN-13: 978-1-933337-23-4
ISBN-10: 1-933337-23-0
10 9 8 7 6 5 4 3 2 1

TO THE MEMORY OF
SAM HOUSTON
AND HIS CO-PATRIOTS

Jeff Hamilton in 1934. Etching by Bernhardt Wall from a photograph by Temple Houston Morrow. *Courtesy of The Center for American History of the University of Texas at Austin.*

FOREWORD

It has been a long time since I enjoyed reading anything so much as I have the manuscript of *My Master*. These recollections of my grandfather, General Sam Houston, by his ex-slave, Jeff Hamilton, have the same kind of dramatic force and human-interest flavor that made Trader Horn's reminiscences so readable.

Jeff's unique story, however, possesses the advantage of an American setting, and overflows with the patriotic fervor and wholesome philosophy of old-time Americanism.

Dear old Jeff! He is indeed one of my most cherished boyhood memories. He often visited our home at Independence. I see he is just as eager as ever to tell a side-splitting joke on himself or to relate some interesting anecdote concerning General Houston and his political cronies. Nor does he overlook humorous and pathetic happenings in the lives of his fellow-slaves—Uncle Joshua, Tom Blue, Aunt Liza, and his own Mammy, "Aunt Big Kittie."

One marvels that a man of Jeff's years is able to recall so clearly incidents in his early life. It is remarkable how well the old negro understands the important issues that so long agitated the public mind during the days of secession, war, and reconstruction.

Mr. Hunt does an expert job of interviewing and writing. It is something new, this opportunity of seeing a public character through the eyes of his former slave, who is now over one hundred years old. It is also a novel experience to have paraded before us in such a lifelike way people and scenes of the distant past.

My Master is a real contribution to American folklore and history, and I believe that readers everywhere will be as fascinated and entertained by this book as I have been.

FRANKLIN WILLIAMS

Temple Houston Morrow, grandson of Sam Houston, visiting with Jeff Hamilton in Belton, Texas, circa 1935. *Courtesy Railroad & Pioneer Museum, Temple, Texas.*

PREFACE

"That old Negro made the finest address of the day," the president of the Centennial Association of Texas told me on the day following the dedication of a historical marker at the old bayshore home of Sam Houston at Cedar Point. One of the honor guests invited to attend the ceremonies was Jeff Hamilton, Houston's former slave, now over one hundred years old.

"Happily, someone called on Jeff for a few remarks," continued the Centennial official. "He related some of the most astonishing experiences I have ever heard. He recounted, with all the ease and poise of a veteran after-dinner speaker, humorous episodes, campaign yarns, and some of the deadly thunderbolts 'Old Sam' hurled at political enemies.

"We want you to see the old man at once, and save for posterity his rare recollections. You see, he is one of the very few men now living who passed through the hates and passions of the '50s and '60s and who may give us an eyewitness picture of life and conditions in that eventful era."

I accepted the assignment with enthusiasm. Here, I felt, was an opportunity to tap a virgin source of pioneer reminiscences. From this observant centenarian, I might obtain new and startling viewpoints on the institution of slavery, secession, and the bitter conflict between the American states. From the lips of Jeff Hamilton I might coax intimate and revealing sidelights on the life and philosophy of the boldest figure in an age noted for its hardihood and courage.

On a fine Spring morning I stopped my car at the foot of a hillside overlooking the beautiful city of Belton, Texas.

Climbing terraced steps to the lawn above, I faced a cozy cottage. In front of the house towered two great oaks, under which sat old Jeff and his dog Trip, a Boston bull-terrier. The Negro patriarch welcomed me warmly. With joyous barks, Trip entered into the spirit of the greeting.

"Yessiree, Mr. Hunt," said Jeff, as I handed him letters of introduction from Centennial officials and a grandson of Houston, "I'm proud to meet you, an' glad t' know from your letter the other day you're goin' to help me write my 'memoirs' as they call them."

While Jeff was reading my "credentials," I observed the arrangements he had made for the task ahead of us.

Between the trees he had placed a table and two old-fashioned rocking chairs. On the table stood a pitcher of ice-water and several of Jeff's old pipes, which I soon learned he much preferred to the "segars" I had brought him. Lina, his daughter, with whom he lives, was piling at his feet his favorite books on Texas and his hero—Sam Houston. In his lap lay pages of notes which were frayed and yellowed by age.

The small, sinewy man, who appeared not a day over eighty, won my admiration quickly. His personality radiated charm, humor, and sincerity. A disarming smile always lit up his features, upon which the years had left few wrinkles. His eyes were remarkably clear, and looked at me directly in a friendly, half-quizzical way. Jeff had never gone to school a day in his life, but had educated himself fairly well. His voice was pleasing, with its soft drawl. He spoke the colloquial language of Texas, but, in describing some exciting experience, he often lapsed into the idiom of his own race.

I picked up Jeff's cane to examine the ornate carvings upon it.

"That old cane of mine is jus' like my master's favorite walking stick he toted in his old age," he explained. "My rheumatics gets so bad sometimes I've got t' use it lookin' after my garden, chickens, and hogs.

"I guess you won't believe a lot of things I'll tell you," continued Jeff. "An' you'll never find in th' history books a great deal more I recollects about my master an' the missus an' the childr'n an' his fight against the slavers an' secessionists. Don't let me forget to tell you about Uncle Joshua, my master's blacksmith. An' there's Tom Blue, his coachman, too, who escaped over into Mexico with another slave."

The old fellow proved to be a good story teller. He wandered from his subject at times, but seemed to appreciate the attention of a good listener. I realized at once that his recital would surpass in interest and realism synthetic memories by professional ghost writers.

"Did you know," Jeff went on, "that when I was a littl' child my owner was a regular Simon Legree sort of man an' a drunkard an' took me away from my Mammy —who they calls 'Aunt Big Kittie' she was so large—an' auction'd me off on the slave-block t' pay a bill for two barrels of whiskey? He also sold Mammy an' the rest of th' childr'n an' scatters 'em all over Texas, so I didn't see'm again for over twenty-five years!

"I've always thanked my Maker that He had General Houston drive up when I was standin' on the slave-block at Huntsville that hot day in the fall of 1853, an' that he bought me to play with his own little son.

"There was a real man for you—one of that kind of leaders who had a mind of his own on slavery an' secession an' everythin' else, an' who believed in treatin' us slaves like we're human beings!

"An' who'd ev'r tho't in those days that an ignorant little Negro like me from the backwoods would get t' be the servant, driver, an' office boy of a man like my master?

"Yessiree, I drove him in his old top buggy all over Texas when he was a United States senator an' also when he made two campaigns for governor of Texas.

"I heard almost all his speeches, an' met most of the other big statesmen an' business men he knew durin' that time, an' many a night I sat an' listens to their jokes an' their quarrels over states' rights.

"After my master had to give up the office of governor because he wouldn't take the oath of the Confederate nation, I saw him two or three times with secession mobs all 'round him who swore they'd hang him if he dar'd make a speech. But he spoke everywhere alright, threats or no threats, as he was the bravest man that ev'r lived.

"Why, I saved my master one night from being murder'd by two of his worst political enemies, an' I saw with my own eyes the letter Mr. Lincoln wrote my master jus' before he was president, offerin' to make him a general in the Army of the North an' then send him fifty thousan' soldiers by ships so he could put down secession in Texas an' help Mr. Lincoln save our Union.

"I always slep' on a pallet jus' outside my master's door. But for a long time before he died he'd have me put my pallet by his own bed so I could get anythin' he wanted. I've seen him an' talked with him in my dreams more times than I can tell since he died," concluded the loyal old fellow with a display of inherent African mysticism.

Jeff was now tiring, and welcomed my suggestion that we adjourn our first session to meet again the following morning.

I had taken down every word Jeff uttered, and he was curious to see the shorthand notes. I read him several pages of his "dictation," a feat which impressed him so much I began to hope the ex-slave might regard an ex-court reporter as a man of importance.

It was agreed that Jeff would turn over to me such of his "memoirs" as he had put in writing, and that each morning I would take down other recollections he might recall. He seemed much pleased that I would then edit the whole mass of material and "place it in book English," preserving at many places, however, Jeff's own inimitable word-for-word narrartion.

As I prepared to leave, Jeff entrusted his "manuscript" to my keeping. A little reluctantly, I sensed, did he relinquish his most treasured possession, judging from his wistful, far-away look, as if he were trying to turn back Time eighty-five years to the beginning of his association with his beloved master. With the roll of pencilled notes, I found an old-timey scrapbook, which proved to be a priceless thing.

Jeff must have thought it proper to give me a history of the documents he handed me—perhaps, unconsciously, he wished to indulge his sense of humor.

"Mr. Hunt, I told you awhile ago I'd never gone to school a single day," said Jeff, "but I forgot to tell you I went t' college nigh on t' fifteen years, an' almos' got a degree.

"It all happens this way: Do you see about two blocks off from where we're sittin' those fine school buildin's an' magnif'c'nt groun's that looks jus' like a park? Well, that's Hardin-Baylor Female Coll'ge, which is one of the oldes' an' greates' schools in America. I was janitor there for over fo'teen years from 1889 until almos' 1904.

"The professors gave me all th' books I wanted from the library, an' I read more and got more book learnin' there than in all my life, befo' or since. One year at commencm'nt time, one of the famous divines of the country made the address, an' the president of the school points me out to him, an' says:

" 'Jeff here is the best pupil we've got, an' will soon finish his pos' graduate work in Texas history and English.'

"The funny part of it was the preacher was a northern man, an' didn't know 'twas all a joke, at first.

"Anyhow, it's right there that I begun writin' down all I could remember about my slave days an' the war an' 'mancipation, an' also about my master, the missus an' the childr'n."

I drove at once to my hotel, impatient to examine under the historical writer's microscope the outcrop from the rich mother-lode of folk-lore and human drama I had just prospected.

I took stock of my good fortune. I was grateful that the president of the Centennial Association had fired my imagination with the possibilities embodied in Jeff and his recollections. I was now glad that Houston's descendants had strongly urged me to undertake the mission to the home of this remarkable man.

I read page after page of Jeff's unique chronicle. He seemed to follow no chronology, but rambled from incident to incident, with surprising clarity of expression, however. His observations ranged from the most trivial matters to political debates that rocked the nation. The material before me would have made happy the heart of the most tireless delver into musty things of the past.

As I lay aside the data for the night, I felt elated that for several weeks I would be able to talk face to face with their author, who had walked beside the colossal figure of Sam Houston as he strode across the American stage. I now knew that Jeff would give me picturesque details of Houston's rugged showmanship on the stump and of his conquests as frontier soldier, statesman, and diplomat. I thrilled over the rare privilege to cross-examine an actual eyewitness to the drama, romance, and tragedy which had crowded the lives of master and servant during the most critical and tempestuous period in our country's history. It was satisfying to reflect that I might hear the honest opinions of an ingenuous observer, with the uncanny ability to make keen appraisals of men and events and their meaning to history.

Yes, I had found a guileless old soul who could give me from an entirely new angle a simple account of the stirring times in which he lived. I had found an aged Boswell anxious to tell the inside story of the colorful empire-maker who had liberated a people and who directly and indirectly had added over a million square miles to the area of the United States.

I promised myself that on the morrow I would report early at the open-air office under the trees which my colleague had provided for our work and comfort.

LENOIR HUNT

1556 Castle Court, Houston, Texas
November 1, 1940

TABLE OF CONTENTS

LIST OF ILLUSTRATIONS

PUBLISHER'S NOTE

The author has preserved for this and future generations, the recollections of an interesting old man which it is believed will be a valuable addition to the romantic formative years of Texas history. This work gives the human side of a giant of the frontier, who is probably the most colorful character in the annals of America.

Jeff Hamilton was purchased by General Sam Houston in Huntsville, Texas, as he stood on a slave block, a frightened boy of thirteen years. As the slave, body servant and office boy of the Governor of Texas, covering a period of ten years, he had a rare opportunity of observing the private and public life of a great public servant.

Although now over 100 years old, Jeff Hamilton's memory is remarkably clear and his account of the incidents of that important period in Texas and American history is both interesting and informative.

At the end of several chapters, the author gives an intelligent historical background for the recollections, with interesting verbatim comments of Old Jeff himself.

For obvious reasons, the names of some of the personages described in the narrative have been changed.

South Fifth Street home in Temple, Texas, where Jeff Hamilton lived with his second wife, Alice Morris, circa 1912-1928.

Chapter I

"A LITTLE NIGGER FOR SALE – CHEAP!"

My first and most vivid recollection is that of my Mammy. She was such a huge woman that she was called "Aunt Big Kittie." Often, she told me that I was born in old Kentucky on the plantation of Mr. Singleton Gibson and his wife, Mrs. Bettie Gibson, located in the heart of the blue grass country.

Even after the lapse of nearly one hundred years, I remember how Mammy always liked to talk about the Gibson's fine colonial home. She said the slave cabins were comfortable and nicely furnished and that our owners were "quality aristocrats" from Virginia, who treated their slaves with kindness. Having a big appetite, Mammy would smack her lips and speak in glowing terms of the plentiful supply of good food given the slaves.

It seems when I was three years old, Mr. and Mrs. Gibson kept hearing such wonderful stories about the new Texas Republic that they sold their plantation and moved with their slaves to Fort Bend County, Texas, which was a wild frontier country, and bad luck followed our owners everywhere. As a final calamity, Mr. Gibson was killed in an expedition against the Indians.

After Mr. Gibson died, Mrs. Gibson married a Mr. McKell. Her friends begged her not to marry him. They said he was a "rolling stone" and jack of all trades. But

Mr. McKell was a very handsome man and with his plausible ways overcame all the objections of Mrs. Gibson's friends.

And what I tell you about my cruel owner is not because I now bear him any hate on account of his mistreatment of my mother and her children. Even if I cannot forget it, I have forgiven him all that long ago, and want only to give the real facts as I remember them.

I recall our new master and mistress moved from place to place after their marriage until at last they settled in the backwoods of Trinity County, a few miles west of Old Sumpter, which was then the county-seat.

Mr. McKell built a two-room house with a lean-to. It was set on posts driven into the ground and weatherboarded with four-foot boards. It was unpainted like most of the farm houses in those days.

Mr. McKell let his place run down, and rarely made a good crop. He drank and gambled all the time down on Trinity River, where there was always a crowd of the toughest characters in Texas. He had sold or lost at cards all but about ten of his slaves. We slaves lived in miserable huts which he called "cabins." We were worked long hours, whipped, cursed, and half-starved by our new master.

Mr. McKell was justice of the peace for awhile until the better class of people got to know him and learned that he broke the law oftener than many of the criminals he tried.

The first preaching I ever heard was at Mr. McKell's place. A Methodist circuit rider by the name of Reverend

Mr. Seat rode up to the house one day. My master's conscience must have been hurting him, as he had been drinking hard for about a week, and so he asked the preacher to stay all night and hold services. There was no room in the little house for the slaves, so we stood outside the house by an open window.

Before the sermon was finished, a storm came up and blew the roof off the house. No one was hurt, but the wind carried all the quilts and feather-beds into the yard. The trees and the ground looked like they were covered with snow. While we slaves were cleaning up the yard, Mr. McKell was cursing us and his bad luck right before the minister and his own wife.

I was a small, puny boy of thirteen, but, if I should live a thousand years, I would never forget my awful experiences on that day in 1853 when I was torn away from my Mammy and auctioned off on the slave-block to pay an overdue bill for two barrels of whiskey!

Long before daylight on the morning of the auction, Mr. McKell came to our cabin. He pounded on the door. Mammy woke me, my brother, and two sisters, and told us to get up and dress at once.

"Send Jeff over to the house right away," Mr. McKell hollered. "The rest of you hurry up and get to your cotton picking!"

My mother was a fast worker, in spite of her great size, and in a few minutes we were eating our breakfast of sow-belly and corn-bread. As she leaned over the fire-place — stoves were practically unknown in Texas at that time — I could see the fear in Mammy's face. All of us

were deathly afraid of Mr. McKell, and we all knew that
he was drunk the night before. I am sure Mammy thought
he was going to whip me for something he imagined I
had done, or may have thought something worse would
happen.

As I was leaving the cabin, Mammy hugged me and
kissed me good-bye. You see, I was her favorite child
because I was so frail and sickly.

As I ran toward the tumble-down barn, I turned my
head for one last look at my mother. She was standing
in the cabin door, holding her apron to her face and
sobbing in a kind of hopeless way. I was not to see her
again for a quarter of a century. Soon, she and the rest
of the children would be sold separately, and scattered
all over Texas.

Two men slaves were waiting in the wagon, one of
them holding the reins. Mr. McKell ordered me roughly
to "pile in." As the wheels began to roll, I started to
whimper, but the black scowl upon my master's face
hushed me at once.

Riding in a big wagon pulled by two fast mules was
such an unusual experience that I forgot my troubles for
a time. The road was only a trail through the dense
jungles of the Trinity bottoms. But soon we reached the
beautiful rolling hills and valleys and found ourselves in
the town of Huntsville.

At the courthouse square, Mr. McKell stopped the
wagon and ordered the two slaves to pick up the big
slave-block. Covered with dust and sweat, my master
swore at the slaves as they carried the auction block across

the street and placed it beside the plank-walk in front of
the T. & S. Gibbs' store, where most of the traders could
always be found.

Then, with an impatient wave of his hand, Mr. McKell
motioned to me to get up on the slave-block. I was scared
almost to death, but did as he told me. At the top of his
voice, my master cried out time and time again:

"Here's a little nigger for sale — cheap!"

That was eighty-six years ago, and I was, of course, that
little "nigger."

Auctions of slaves were held almost every day in those
times. Yet they always brought together a lot of people.
And so, when I was being sold, a big crowd had gathered
in front of the Gibbs' general store, where the bank now
stands. I looked everywhere trying to find some friendly
face, black or white. I was frightened — scared almost to
death.

The sun beat down on my bare head without mercy.
I was hot, tired, thirsty, and hungry. My misery was made
worse by the sight of a pile of ginger-bread in the store
window a few feet from where I was standing on the
slave-block.

I do not know why Mr. McKell acted as his own auc-
tioneer, unless he wanted to save the usual fees. The
auction dragged, and I began to cry.

"Make me a bid on this little nigger. He is a strong and
willing worker," said Mr. McKell. "He's only eight years
old, and will make a husky field-hand!"

I never knew why Mr. McKell falsified my age unless
he thought he could not sell a runty, small-fry boy like

myself if bidders knew I was thirteen years old instead of eight. There were already too many house-boys and gardeners, and if a buyer knew my real age, he would know that I would never grow into a big, strong slave.

I stood on the slave-block in the blazing sun for at least two hours. The late October day was so hot Mr. McKell had been forced to take off his coat and vest. It was long past noon. My legs ached. My hunger had become almost unbearable. I had been tied to my mother's apron-strings all my life, and had never before seen so many strange people at one time. I was filled with terror, and did not know what was to become of me.

I had been crying for a long time. A lot of white boys had stopped by the block, and they were teasing me and laughing at me. Every time one of them pointed his finger at me and acted like he was going to hit me, I howled with fear. I am sure no criminal on a scaffold was ever more miserable than I was on that hot October day.

At last, Mr. McKell got a bid for me. It was made by a man by the name of Moreland, who offered $500. After dickering for awhile, Mr. McKell took the offer. But he said the deal would have to be closed in time for him to get back home before night. Mr. Moreland lived a few miles below Huntsville. Getting on his horse, he rode away, promising to be back with the money in a couple of hours.

Just as Mr. Moreland galloped down the street in a cloud of dust, a large and important-looking man drove up in a buckboard buggy, drawn by a fine black horse. My eyes opened wide. Never before had I seen a buggy!

"A Little Nigger for Sale — Cheap!"

Stepping down to the ground, the tall man tied his reins to a hitching-post in front of the plank-walk. I saw that he was about six feet two inches high.

"What's all this excitement about?" he asked.

Someone in the crowd answered:

"Nothing at all, General. Just a little nigger boy being sold."

Two keen yet kindly blue eyes looked at me. For some reason, a thrill of awe and wonder ran through me, and I could not keep my eyes from the strange and powerful person who towered above me. I was to learn later that I was gazing for the first time at General Sam Houston, the friend of President Andrew Jackson and the Hero of San Jacinto. My chance meeting with him was to change the whole course of my life.

The man called "General" walked up to Mr. McKell and said:

"My friend, don't you know it is against the law to block the plank-walk in this way? If you want to put on a show, why don't you move the slave-block back to the courthouse square where it belongs?"

Mr. McKell started to say something, when the General cut him short, and said:

"This little Negro isn't old enough to have any sense, and these white boys are scaring him. What sort of offer have you had for the boy, anyway? Has he a father or mother?"

My owner then explained about the offer he had, and said that I had a mother and a brother and two sisters.

"Do you mean to tell me," shouted General Houston,

"that you would take this half-starved child away from his mother and sell him to a yellow dog like Moreland?"

Mr. McKell answered that his creditors would close him out if he didn't settle two whiskey bills the next day, and that he would sell me to anybody who would pay him $500, although I was worth more.

The General then looked Mr. McKell straight in the face, saying:

"McKell, I wouldn't be guilty of separating the family. Rather than see this happen and let this little fellow fall into the hands of a slave-driver like Moreland, I'll take him myself, if you will knock $50 from the price, and sell me the rest of the family, too."

Mr. McKell thought the matter over and then answered:

"Well, General, it's a bargain. You pay me $450 cash right now and I will also sell you the boy's ma, 'Aunt Big Kittie,' and the other children at any price Bolivar Sublett over at Trinity Ferry puts on them."

It seems that Mr. Sublett was known everywhere as an expert on the value of African slaves. Remember that the law then made Negro slaves "property," and that many white people looked upon us colored folks as animals just like a horse or a cow. Mr. Sublett did about the same work as a mule-buyer or stock-yard inspector or appraiser does today, and figured a slave's worth on age, sex, and strength to work.

My new master then lifted me off the block and took me into the Gibbs store.

"Tom," he said to the store-man, "give this little rascal

something to eat. I expect he will eat more than he is worth by the time he grows up. I'll be back soon. Draw up a bill of sale for $450, and when McKell signs it, pay him and charge the money to my account."

For the second time that day my eyes opened wide in amazement. I was standing in a store for the first time in my life!

Everywhere I looked I saw counters and shelves crammed with what seemed to me an unbelievable quantity of goods. There were all kinds of boxes, cans, and barrels, and sacks of coffee and salt. Stacked on platforms were big rows of bacon and pork which almost reached the ceiling.

Mr. Gibbs gave me something to eat, which tasted mighty good to a hungry boy, but the food was new and strange except the ginger-cakes.

When my new master came back, he took me over to a counter, picked out a white straw hat, with a long red streamer, and put it on my head. I was the proudest boy alive, as that was the first "store-bought" hat I ever had. Then, he stopped at one of the show-cases, filled a paper sack with stick candy, and handed it to me, saying in the friendliest kind of way:

"Jeff, you little squirrel, stay here and eat your candy. Don't get scared and cry any more, as nobody is going to hurt you. Joshua will come for you. I have a little boy almost as old as you with whom you can play."

The very sound of my master's voice swept away my fears. From that time on, he was my hero and I was his loyal slave. I played around the store as I pleased, and the hours passed quickly. Only once or twice did I get homesick for "Aunt Big Kittie."

Many cowboys, farmers, and people from the town came in the store to buy, or to barter their chickens, eggs, pecans, and honey. Some came only to gossip with fat, jolly "Mr. Tom" about crops or politics. A few "free Negroes" drifted in. These former slaves had made enough money by extra work to buy their freedom or had been freed by their owners for long and faithful service. I overheard Mr. Gibbs tell some one that I was a lucky little devil to have caught the fancy of a man like "Old Sam."

Uncle Joshua, the blacksmith, came for me a little before sundown. I learned afterwards that he was my master's most trusted slave and straw-boss of the other slaves. His first duty was to keep the General's horses and mules shod and the buggy, coach, and wagons in good shape, after which my master allowed him to work for Colonel Grant, owner of the stage-lines, and keep the money he made. At my master's death, Uncle Joshua had saved over $2,000 in gold.

I liked Uncle Joshua from the start. He was a very large, good-natured man past middle age. On the way home, he teased me about my new "Sunday hat," saying that nobody but little girls wore hats with red ribbons hanging from them.

General Houston lived fourteen miles from Huntsville, and called his home Raven Hill. The "Raven" was the name the Indian chief had given my master when he adopted him as his own son.

"A Little Nigger for Sale — Cheap!"

And that was the way I happened to become the slave of General Sam Houston. I had never gone to school a day, had never had a hat or a pair of shoes, and knew nothing of the ordinary things of life. I could not then know that on that day Fate had taken "a little nigger" from the auction block to make him the trusted servant of a great leader, one who believed in the just and humane treatment of my people.

Even had I known my future, with my narrow outlook I would have been unable to appreciate how I would later thrill over the wonderful privilege of driving my master all over Texas in his old top buggy in his two bitter campaigns for governor — how I would glory in his great fight against secession and for our Union.

Actually, I was to become the office boy of the governor of Texas! I was to hear many of my master's famous stories, and was to see with my own eyes politicians, statesmen, generals, and big business men who helped make Texas and our whole nation what they are today.

As I got out of the wagon to open the gate for Uncle Joshua, I could not realize, of course, that I was standing on the threshold of years of tense drama — yes, and stark tragedy, too!

Likeness of Jeff Hamilton reproduced from a painting by Warren Hunter, owned in 1940 by Dr. C.H. Langford of Goose Creek, Texas.

Chapter II

LIFE AT RAVEN HILL

That October day in 1853, when Mr. James McKell separated me from my Mammy — Aunt Big Kittie — and auctioned me off from the slave-block to pay two past due whiskey bills, was the longest day of my life of nearly one hundred years.

I had been very nervous all day. Hope, fear, suspense, and an intense homesickness for my mother nearly drove me crazy. I had been standing on the slave-block in front of the Gibbs' store in Huntsville for hours. The sun was blazing hot, and when I saw General Houston ride up in his buggy, I do not believe that my small, aching legs could have held me up many minutes longer. Then, came my deliverance from a cruel and inhuman master.

But, sitting in the wagon beside Uncle Joshua, as we drove up to Raven Hill, General Houston's plantation home fourteen miles from Huntsville, I felt safe from the anguish and the terrors of the horrible nightmare of the morning.

From Uncle Joshua's cabin in the slave-quarters, I could see the lights from many candles shining brightly through the windows of my new master's home which he had built in 1844.

After the "white folks" had eaten their supper, Uncle Joshua went to the kitchen, which was connected with

[13]

the main house by a covered porch or kind of runway, and got some food for me from Aunt Liza. As I started to eat, many of the other slaves crowded into the cabin. All of them were talking at once and looking me over from head to foot. But huge Uncle Joshua, seeing how frightened I was and knowing how tired and homesick I must be, ran them out of the house.

From one of the cabins, I could hear notes of a banjo, and a good clear voice singing:

"Rose! Rose! my coal-black Rose!
I nebber seen a nigger dat I lub like Rose!"

I tried to keep awake, but I was soon fast asleep on a pallet Uncle Joshua had spread for me near his own bed.

We awoke early the next morning. It was a clear, beautiful day. Across the road from the cabin, which was one of about a dozen strung out in row, stood the blacksmith shops, barns, and horse and cow lots. Near the shop was a deep well, and I watched Uncle Joshua closely as he drew a bucket of water. We washed in the long water-trough, drying our faces and hands with cotton cloths.

Two young slaves named Pearl and Nash were watering a string of ten or fifteen horses and mules at the water-trough alongside the well. Then they took the animals back to Barn No. 1, as the horse and mule stable was called, placed them in their stalls, and fed them the corn they had shucked for them. While they were currying and rubbing the mules and horses, Uncle Joshua had me climb the ladder to the loft and throw down bundle after bundle of fodder to complete their rations.

From the stable, we went to the cow-lot where another

barn was used for the cows and calves. There we found
busy at their milking Creasy and Mary, daughters of Aunt
Mary, one of the housekeepers. The cows were munching
on fodder and cottonseed, mixed with corn meal.

Many years would pass before people were to learn
how rich cottonseed really is in oil, and from that dis-
covery build up the great business of refining cottonseed
oil which now competes with lard and olive oil.

A large pig-pen adjoined the cow-lot. There we found
Princy, who was General Houston's foreman, and who
had almost as much authority as Uncle Joshua. He was
feeding the pigs a plant we called "pusley," the scientific
name of which is "purslane." It was a kind of vine-like
weed that grew wild and spread over everything, and was
worthless except as hog-feed, as the hogs seemed to like
it very much.

It was now breakfast time for all the "hands" on the
place. On our way to the kitchen, we passed by the
garden, which covered more than a block, and next to
the garden was a turnip-patch almost as large. We saw
one of the Negro girls coming from the garden with an
apronful of young radishes and onions.

About twenty feet from the kitchen stood the smoke-
house. "Hog-killing time" came late in the fall after the
weather got cold. In the smoke-house were stored barrels
of sausage and salted pork, while slabs of bacon and hams
were strung from the rafters for "home-curing" over a
slow hickory fire.

A short distance from the house I saw a small, one-
story building which Uncle Joshua explained to me was

[15]

the General's "office," but it was some time before I found out what he meant by the word "office."

I was curious about a box-like affair that looked something like the open body of a truck now used for hauling and dumping sand and gravel. Uncle Joshua explained to me that this was the ash-hopper. The ashes from the fire-places were taken up every morning and thrown in the hopper. When the rains came and wet the ashes, a lye was formed, which dripped into a bucket at the bottom of the hopper. The lye was then mixed with fats from the hogs to make lye soap, which was used for most purposes, especially in washing clothes. You see the fine scented soaps shipped in from the north and from Europe cost so much that only well-to-do white people could afford to use them.

Where there were only a few slaves on a place, it was usual for the slaves to eat in the kitchen instead of cooking their own meals in the slave quarters. It was during my first meal in the kitchen at Raven Hill that something happened which shows the charity and sympathy my master had for his unfortunate slaves.

The regular fare for slaves almost the year round was fat meat, molasses, and corn-bread or hoe-cake, with lots of buttermilk, at times. If we slaves caught an extra big number of opossums, the General would let us keep some, and how we would enjoy these occasional feasts of " 'possum and sweet taters"! But Uncle Joshua told me later that the General fed his slaves much better than most other owners did. He must have been right, for that morning Old Aunt Liza, the cook, and her oldest daughter, Hannah, had filled for us two big platters with a lot of pork, tripe, fried sweet potatoes, and cracklin' bread.

We were all reaching into the platters and eating with our fingers when the door opened, and our master walked in, smiling. But when he saw the awful way in which we were handling the food, the smile left his face.

"Joshua! Liza! What in the h . . . do you mean by letting these people eat like a lot of hogs? You are not living at the home of a savage!"

As he stormed out of the room, he shouted to Uncle Joshua:

"Hitch up my buggy and bring it around to the front with Jeff!"

The General drove at once to Mr. Tom Gibbs' store, in front of which the day before I had been sold from the slave-block.

With the help of Mrs. Gibbs, my master selected a lot of tin plates, knives, forks, spoons, and cups, ordering me to put the packages in his buggy.

The General then sat down on a big dry-goods box and began whittling on a pine board, which I soon found was his favorite habit.

"Come here, Tom, and tell me something," he said to the store-keeper. "Have you any idea how many white people teach their slaves how to eat in civilized fashion, and how many of them do you think there are who do not furnish them with knives, forks, and plates?"

Mr. Gibbs thought a minute and answered:

"Well, General, I guess maybe over half of the people let their slaves eat like animals. Do you remember that a

short time back a big churchman advanced a theory that
the Negro was not a human being but *an animal without
a soul*?"

"But of course," he added, "I do not believe that idea
has anything to do with it. I think most people have never
given the matter any thought, and would have corrected
it long ago if somebody had agitated the question."

I was too young and ignorant to understand the meaning of the long talk between the General and Mr. Gibbs
about slavery, secession, and other things, but, from the
little I did understand and can remember, I got the idea,
and I still believe I am right, that there were three classes
of slave-owners. The first class was as cruel as James
McKell, my former owner; the second was almost as bad,
since they turned over their slaves to hard-boiled bosses;
and the third class were the Christian men like my master.

I do not believe any man ever lived who watched people
and events as closely as I have throughout my long life.
I saw most of the meanness as well as the good things that
were going on about me. I honestly believe that the third
or better class of owners, such as the General, were in the
great majority. They must have amounted to fully seventy-
five per cent of the slave-owners.

As my master did not farm in a big way, he did not
need many slaves. Most of the fourteen slaves he owned
when he bought me he hired out to others to learn a trade,
but he was very particular to hire them to good people.
He raised only enough food and feedstuff for his own
family and his stock. His wealth was mostly in lands and
mortgages.

The General and the Missus saw to it that the cabins were kept neat and clean, and that we had plenty of bed covering during the cold months. We didn't have to run around in our bare feet in the winter-time like many slaves, but were given good shoes and other clothing. The General did not permit his slaves to be whipped. And if we got sick, we had the best care that any one could possibly get in that day and time.

Mrs. Houston was one of the pillars of the Baptist Church. There never was a husband or father in the world who loved his family more than my master did.[1] He had not joined the church when he bought me, but, knowing how his wife felt about religion, and also believing it was a good thing, he gave strict orders that every slave must attend prayer-meeting in the house once a week. On Sundays, the white people went to church in the morning, and the colored people attended services in the afternoon or at night. When the General was at home from Washington, I always went to the church with him to hold his horse, or to take care of his horse and buggy, if he went in that way.

As we took the dishes and other things back home, the General seemed to be in much better humor. On the trip I again became the proudest boy in the world! My master let me hold the reins of the horse part of the way home, which made me feel as proud as I had the day before when he gave me my first hat with the long red streamer. He told me that Uncle Joshua was too valuable a man to quit his other work and drive him around. He said that after I had learned to drive that he might "elect"

[19]

me his "official driver" when he traveled about "politick-ing" and on other business.

As we came within sight of Raven Hill, my master made a statement that showed how much he believed in the education of colored people. He told me that there was no sense in not teaching all the slaves how to read and write and do simple sums. He said he was going to have someone among the colored folk at his place who had some education start a class so that every Negro boy and girl in the community, whether they belonged to him or not, might at least learn how to read and write.

I have always been interested in the question, wanting to see the boys and girls of my race get the education that I failed to get. I have a mass of figures here that I have col-lected which show what the people of Texas have done for colored education. I know that the stand my master took on free public education for all the people and the educational planks in his platform had a big influence on the voters.

It was unpopular for my master to speak in favor of educating Negroes, because most people didn't think it worth while to send a slave child to school, and many of them didn't want to pay taxes to provide free public schools, even for white children. Times were hard, and in 1857 we had one of the worst panics ever known in the United States. The first free public school to open in Texas did not open until 1854 in San Antonio,[2] although I understand that they had been talking about free schools ever since the Texas Republic was established over fif-teen years before.

We saw everybody on the place out by the front gate

when we got back home. The big yellow family coach with its four horses pulling on their bits was standing before the gate. It seems that the General and Mrs. Houston had planned to make a trip to Independence, about fifty miles away, where the General owned another home which he had bought years before and where Mrs. Houston's mother lived.

My mistress was just stepping into the carriage with the two colored maids and her children—Sam, Jr., 10; Nancy Elizabeth, 7; Margaret Lea, 5; Mary Willie, 3; and the baby, Antoinette Power, nearly 2 years old.

Tom Blue, the fine-looking mulatto coachman, whom my master had bought in Washington years before and who would later make a very sensational escape to Mexico, where there was no slavery, got up on the driver's seat and cracked his long whip. The General and I went ahead in his top buggy.

We made good time, as the roads were dry but very dusty. Mrs. Houston suffered from asthma a great deal, and the dust made it worse. When we reached Independence late that afternoon, Mrs. Houston's mother welcomed us as if she hadn't seen her folks for years, and had a fine supper cooked. She was in charge of the Baptist Church, and claimed that Independence was getting to be the best town in Texas for education. Some people called it the "Athens of Texas." Baylor University was located there. It had been chartered by the Texas Republic in 1841, and is now one of the big universities of Texas.

The next morning, the General hunted up his nephew, Major Martin Roysten. He turned over to him some land notes to collect and told him all about me. He asked the major to go and see Mr. McKell at once; as he had no confidence in any promise he made and was afraid that he would sell the rest of my family and separate us forever. This is exactly what happened, and it was over twenty-five years before I saw my mother again. The General explained that he couldn't look after the matter, as he had to go back to the United States Senate in Washington within a few days. The General said that as there were no railroads west of the Mississippi River, it would take him several weeks to reach Washington.

My master then told Major Roysten that he was very much worried about the disputes over slavery. He said that both sides had a great many fanatics and half-crazy people who ought to be muzzled. He said one of the worst things was the way the newspapers, corrupt politicians, and "political preachers" as he called them, were stirring up hate between the two sections. He said that if the real leaders couldn't get together soon, it looked like we would have a senseless war. Such a war he knew would set the country back a hundred years, and wind up with our being divided into a number of little nations, which sooner or later would be gobbled up by foreign countries which hated American institutions.

My master called me and handed me a basket of cakes to put in the back of the buggy. On our trip back to Huntsville, he told me things that I want every patriotic boy and girl in America to hear.

*　*　*　*

"Human slavery was an awful thing, an' it's a good thing it's been outlawed by civilized nations," observed

Jeff when I urged him to give me more details concerning his classification of slave-holders into three groups.

"I know 'cause I was a slave f'r nigh on to twenty-five years. 'Twas the feelin' about it you had that you couldn't do what you wanted to an' not so much the work, as my own work didn't amount t' much, as my master and the missus were sure good to me.

"An' later on, I'll tell you all about how my master freed all his own slaves in '62, the year befo' he died, after he read President Lincoln's proclamation to us, altho' he didn't have to free us at all then accordin' to Texas law.

"Did you know that the first division of slavers like Mr. McKell who was so mean an' cruel to me and my folks was look'd down on and despised by their white neighbors as much as we slaves ourselves hated 'em?

"The secon' class was fine people and good at heart. But they w're men who didn't want t' be bothered with running a big plantation, which was a sure enough job in those days. They liked an easy-like life as officers in the army, or wanted to idle about gamblin', drinkin', horse-racin', fox-huntin', and givin' parties to their swell friends for miles aroun'.

"These two firs' divisions hired bosses and overseers who almos' always had no character or sympathy. They mus' have been a low breed of men who gloried in the brutal power they had over us—like some of the convict guards I've heard about.

"Why, that kind of men didn't let a sick Negro hand quit work in th' field, no matter how hot it was, as long as he could stand on his feet. Sometimes, they whipp'd

[23]

'em without any cause, sayin' they were 'lazy,' 'insubordi-
nate', or tryin' to 'escape,' and would ha' been fired if the
plantati'n owner had known it.

"But, I'm glad that the big majority of slave-owners
were good men like my master. The slaves on his place
were happy, an' just like one big fam'ly."

Sociologists may write learned treatises on slavery and
on master and servant during ante-bellum days and a
decade or two thereafter. Yet, only persons like Jeff and
the numerous "chillun" of a host of dear Old Black
Mammies are able to appreciate the bonds of loyalty and
affection that bound together the whites and the blacks
of the Old South.

Chapter III

HOUSTON BEGINS HIS FIGHT FOR THE UNION

General Houston loved horses and was a good judge of horses. I, too, loved horses, which always proved a strong tie between us. For his buggy horse he had picked out a large, deep-chested sorrel trotter. He named him "Horseshoe," probably because the first battle in which my master fought was Horseshoe Bend in the Creek War under General Andrew Jackson. There he had been badly wounded in the thigh by a barbed arrow and in the right arm and shoulder by an Indian rifle ball.

As I have said before, my master took an interest in everything and everybody about him. During the time I worked for him, I often saw him forget he was a United States Senator, and later throw off his big blanket of governor, as it were. He wanted to relax and get away from his worries and the serious troubles the country faced just before the Civil War.

I sometimes think that he looked upon me as a kind of hobby with which to amuse himself as other great men, I understand, play solitaire or collect books or stamps. He liked to tease me about some trifling thing, or talk to me along a lonely country road while he was turning over in his mind some great thought.

We had left Independence after an early breakfast,

and by eleven-thirty had traveled about half the way to Huntsville. A short distance ahead of us we saw a stream. As we neared the creek, my master said something that showed the influence on his life of the three years he spent with the Cherokees in East Tennessee. It seems that as a boy, my master found school dull and uninteresting, and wanted the excitement and adventure which he might find among his Indian friends, whose head chief adopted him as his own son.

"My boy," the General said, "when you travel, notice everything you pass. There are no two trees alike, just as there are no two bridges or hills or valleys alike. Some time, you may have to make another trip through the same country, and if you remember the landmarks, they will carry you through safely."

When we reached the creek, my master ordered me to unhitch Horseshoe so he could graze in the tall grass. He told me that while the horse was getting his dinner, we would eat, too. The General was very fond of sweet cakes, which were the same as our cookies of today. He asked me to bring to him the basket of cookies which I had put in the buggy, and handed me a handful everytime he helped himself. As we sat on the bank of the creek, he said:

"Jeff, I want to give you a piece of advice, and I want you to promise me that you will follow it, and I believe you will. It is this: You may not always be able to be the most honest and the most truthful man on earth, and there are others who may respect old age as much as you will, but if you try to be honest and truthful and have respect for old people, these three things will carry you through life safely. And if you are loyal to your master, he may free you some day, or you may be able to make enough to buy your freedom."

I have always looked upon his advice as the "three-point star" in my life — my moral code. I have never been arrested or charged with any crime, have never been hobbled like a criminal, nor had handcuffs placed on my wrists. I have never seen the inside of a jail. There are thousands of white and colored men who had far better opportunities than I, who cannot boast of such a record.

What my master meant by my buying my liberty some day was that many slaves often earned money by working overtime on Sundays or during the busy crop season. Their owners let some of them grow a little cotton or raise hogs, cattle, or chickens. Sometimes a slave-owner would make provision in his will granting freedom to one or more of his slaves as a reward for faithful service or for some act of heroism benefiting some member of the owner's family.

Congress was to meet in December, and a few days before the General started for Washington he took me over to Dr. Rawlings' home. The doctor had agreed to hire me at a few dollars a month and teach me the duties of a house-servant — what you would now call butler and valet.

My work was light, as all I had to do was to help with the house and yard work, and with the milking, gardening, and caring for the chickens. Dr. Rawlings and his family treated me kindly. Sam Houston, Jr., was about three years younger than I, but as there were very few boys of his age in the neighborhood, he often came over to the doctor's house to see me and sometimes asked the doctor to let me stay a few days at Raven Hill. We soon became fast friends, playing all sorts of games and getting into mischief like all boys.

Of all the many wonders I saw in this new world of peace and happiness, none equalled in grandeur the piano Mrs. Houston had brought to Texas from Alabama, after her marriage in 1840. For years, it was the only piano in the Texas wilderness. I have seen many men, women, and children come for miles just to see that piano and hoping that they could hear Mrs. Houston or one of her little girls play it. It sounds strange now, but very few of these people had ever seen a piano or heard one played.

There has never been any doubt in my mind about the way Mrs. Houston worshipped her husband. That was one reason, I guess, why she told several people that she married him because she could "reform" him. Up to the time of his marriage in 1840, he was a hard drinker and one of the champion "cussers" of the Southwest. Judge John H. Reagan wrote that when my master married, he stopped his drinking completely, and tried very hard to quit using profane words.

In those days, drinking among men was the rule, rather than the exception as today. The General had drunk so much while he was a Cherokee chieftain for a few years before coming to Texas, that his Indian friends began to call him "Big Drunk."[1]

Of course, his political enemies always accused him of being a heavy drinker, even after he had given up his bad habit.

All of his enemies — and remember that a strong, independent man like my master had plenty of people who hated him — tried to make capital out of the fact that he had married the beautiful widow, Tiana Rogers, who was a real Cherokee princess. Mrs. Tiana Rogers (her people had assumed an American name) was a very fine woman, and it was a case of love at first sight between her and the General.

The marriage between my master and the Indian princess took place soon after he reached Arkansas, after his resignation as Governor of Tennessee. He had been married to Miss Eliza Allen only a few months when, on account of their different natures, they separated. Whenever any one dared to ask my master about the matter, he gave him such a look that he quickly changed the subject. If some close friend mentioned the unfortunate affair, however, he would quietly say, "my lips are sealed."[2]

As to my master's drinking and swearing, I can truthfully say that I never saw him drunk in my life, and rarely heard him utter a profane word. The only time he ever took a drink, which was usually a little bitters with orange peel, was during a wet, cold spell, and when he did this, he generally ordered that the slaves be given some spirits.

At last, my mistress and her mother prevailed upon my master to join the church. On November 19, 1854, about a year after he had bought me from Mr. McKell, he joined the Baptist Church at Independence. I think the sermon was preached by the Reverend Mr. Morrell, who had been a friend and a neighbor of the General and his mother back in Blount County, Tennessee. After the sermon, the Reverend Rufus C. Burleson, who was one of the ancestors of Postmaster-General Albert S. Burleson during President Wilson's term, baptised my master in Rocky Creek not far from the church.[3]

One of those cold snaps had begun to blow before the church services were over. It was a regular "blue Texas norther." Both my master and the Reverend Mr. Burleson looked to me like they were about to freeze to death, as their teeth were chattering when they came out of the chilly waters.

Judge Reagan used to tell a good story about how hard my master tried to quit his habit of cursing. The Judge, the General, and a Baptist preacher were riding along the road one day, soon after my master was converted and baptised, when the General's horse stumbled and almost threw him over his head.

My master shouted, "God d - - - a stumbling horse!"

The preacher couldn't believe his ears, and asked in astonishment, "Brother Houston, do you still swear?"

"Well, what must I do?" asked the General.

"Ask God to forgive you!"

"I will if you'll hold my bridle reins."

The General got off his horse, took off his hat, kneeled down in a fence corner and prayed in the hot sun.[4]

On his political speaking trips, sometimes Joshua drove my master, and sometimes I was his driver. Often, he would drive the buggy himself. Many times he would go out of his way to pick up one of his close political friends or some old army veteran he knew at San Jacinto or in the Creek Wars under General Jackson in Tennessee, so that they could talk over election plans and old times as well.

[30]

No matter how hot the weather, my master invariably wore a large, soft-brimmed fur hat, and a vest made out of leopard's skin during his speech-making tours. He wore no necktie, and left his shirt unbuttoned at the collar. About his tall body of six feet and two inches, he wore a linen duster, which he also left unbuttoned.

Although he was now sixty-four years old, the General still stood as erect as an Indian. He was forced to limp a little, and to use his walking cane at times on account of his ankle having been shattered at the battle of San Jacinto. He told me once when I was dressing it that the doctors in New Orleans took from his ankle twenty-three pieces of bone. He also said that no one on earth would ever know what agony he suffered from his wounded ankle for two or three months after the battle. The arrow wound in his thigh and the rifle ball wounds in his arm and shoulder also troubled him greatly. They never healed, and I had to dress them nearly every day.

My master was one of the finest-looking men who ever stood before a crowd. He was very dignified in his appearance, and his powerful body showed great strength. His face and head were large and well-shaped. His eyes were blue. His voice was deep, firm, and pleasing. He talked slowly and distinctly, having what might be called a "carrying" voice which could be heard by everyone in the largest crowds. He had no campaign manager, and relied on old friends to arrange the details of his speaking, and the barbecue which usually followed political talks. A speaker's stand was usually made by placing two wagons side by side and putting boards or seats in the wagons so General Houston's committee of welcome and old soldier friends might have a place to sit comfortably.

At last in, 1857, my master began his campaign for the governorship of Texas.

There was one incident in the race that I remember distinctly, which was not only dramatic but almost ended in a tragedy. I have since read an account of it written by another eye-witness, Judge A. W. Terrell of Austin, who was a famous lawyer and Minister to Turkey under President Cleveland. He was a member of the Democratic Executive Committee and opposed the General, but afterwards became one of his close friends.[5]

During his speech at Lockhart, in his campaign for governor of Texas, as an independent against the Democratic nominee, Mr. H. R. Runnels, the General saw Judge O. S. Williamson ride up on his horse and take from his saddle bags two volumes of the Congressional Record. There was some commotion, and General Houston said:

"Be still, my friends, be still . . . It's Williamson, only Williamson . . . he is opening some books, but they are not the bank books he stole and sunk in the White River in Arkansas!"

The air was tense, and Judge Williamson was so angry that Judge Terrell says in his article that he bit his cigar in two. Everybody knew that two brave men were facing each other, and they expected firing to begin. Probably the only reason Judge Williamson didn't draw his six-shooter was because he knew General Houston's old friends would kill him if he made a move, and maybe the truth hurt.

My master then looked Judge Williamson over again,

saying that Williamson's name headed a paper issued by the State Executive Committee of which the Judge was chairman. Looking very serious, my master pulled out a pair of buckskin gloves, put them on, and then picked up a copy of the paper, saying:

"The Committee says on this paper that they intended to handle me without gloves. Well, that paper is too dirty for me to handle *without gloves*. It states that all traitors should be defeated, and that in my defeat 'add to theirs a name of fear that traitor knaves shall quake to hear.' "

Letting the paper drop to the floor of the wagon, the General rose to his full height and shouted:

"What! I, a traitor to Texas! I, who in defense of her soil moistened it with my blood?"

Then, he read the names of the executive committee which issued the paper.

"O. S. Williamson — though he stole and sunk those bank books in White River and ran away to Texas, is not yet in a penitentiary!

"J. M. Steiner — a murderer. He murdered Major Arnold. [It was afterwards disclosed that Steiner, who was a cultured gentleman, slew in self-defense and was acquitted by a jury.]

"John Marshall — a vegetarian; he won't eat meat; one drop of his blood would freeze a frog!

"A. W. Terrell — he used to be a Whig in Missouri. They tell me that young scapegrace wants to be a judge. A pretty-looking judge he would make, this slanderer of a man old enough to be his father."

Judge Terrell says in this article that he had heard all

[33]

the great orators of the Republic and State of Texas, but that General Houston beat them all.

There were no trains or telegraph lines in Texas in those days, and it was almost two weeks after the election before the final returns got to Huntsville, showing that Mr. Runnels had won by a vote of 32,552 to 23,628 votes for my master. The General received the news as he sat on the steps of the gallery, carving for one of his little boy friends an Indian head upon a piece of soft white pine.

As he got up to go into the house, he said to his wife: "Margaret, wait until 1859!"

I followed him into the living room. He went over to a table and picked up a big book and began turning the pages. I heard him say something about "liberty and union," and saw him turn down the page he was reading, but it was two or three years before I understood just what he was driving at. One day, when I was cleaning the room, I ran across the same book and opened it at the page he had turned down. He had turned to one of Daniel Webster's speeches in Congress. He admired Webster more than any of the orators and statesmen except General Jackson, whom he put ahead of everybody.

* * * * *

"It beats anythin' I ev'r saw," said Jeff, "the way you can take down what I say and then write it off on your typewriter!"

The art of stenography and typing seemed to fascinate the old man, who was much pleased when I brought a typewriter to our unique "office" under the trees. Each day I was more amazed at Jeff's familiarity with American and Texas history.

With Jeff sitting proudly beside the machine, I transcribed some of the notes I had made covering the momentous events leading up to secession, and Sam Houston's almost single-handed fight to keep Texas within the Union.

A few years prior to secession of the Southern States, there had been little agitation in Texas over slavery and secession. Slave-labor was confined principally to plantations in South and East Texas. The majority of North Texans had come from "free" states, while the numerous Germans of Southwest Texas always had done their own work. The ranches could not profitably work slaves, as it was an easy matter for them to escape into "free" Mexico, which did not recognize slavery.

Henry Clay, the "Great Compromiser," had forestalled open hostilities between warring factions by a long series of "peace treaties." He had successfully sponsored the Missouri Compromise of 1820, the Tariff Compromise Act of 1833 (designed to "nullify" South Carolina's Ordinance of Nullification) and lastly, the famous Compromise of 1850.

But Senator Stephen A. Douglas, the "little giant," in 1854, in an ambitious reach for the presidency, sought to gain the support both of Northern and Southern Democrats with his Kansas-Nebraska Bill. Under this bill, territories yet to become states by popular vote (called by the Senator "popular sovereignty" and "non-intervention"

[35]

and by its enemies "squatter sovereignty") might either legalize or outlaw slavery within their borders.

From that time on until the historic shot on Fort Sumter, the whole nation was rocked by the thunder from Congressional debates on states' rights and secession.

With the vision of a prophet, United States Senator Sam Houston pictured the evils that would follow in the wake of this bill, among which, he said, would be the destruction of the compromise acts mentioned above.

In the knowledge that he was signing his own political death warrant in Texas, the courageous Houston, with his Jacksonesque love of the Union, threw the shining lance of his logic against the foreheads of his defamers, crying:

"The Union — it must and shall be preserved . . . I adjure you to regard the contract once made to harmonize and preserve the Union. *Maintain the Missouri Compromise!* Stir not up *agitation.* Give us peace!"[6]

Houston was blacklisted in Texas mass meetings, in Texas newspapers, and by the Texas Legislature. He realized the strength of the opposition he faced and believed he might better fight the secession movement in Texas as its governor than as a member of the United States Senate.

Chapter IV

EXCITING CAMPAIGN DAYS

"I was now gettin' old enough an' had learn'd enough by lisen'ng to talks the General had with his frien's to understan' somethin about the questions dividin' him and the secession leaders," the talkative old Jeff said one morning almost before I had found my accustomed place under the trees.

"Yessiree, my master seem'd so glad t' see the interes' I took in his 'politickin,' he us'd to call it, an' that I ask'd him all kinds of questions about the 'issues.'

"He was worryin' hims'lf a lot about Horseshoe, his buggy horse I told you about. He had a mighty sore foot, an' none of us on the place was able to cure it. My master was in a big hurry to start out on his secon' race for governor agains' Govern'r Runnels who beat him two years befo' in 1857. I remembers he said he felt he's sure to win. He didn't like to do it, but he tells me to hitch up his fine black mare to the buggy, an' get ready to leave at once."

It was one of those rare Texas days in June, and Jeff was in fine fettle, conversationally speaking, although his rheumatism and deafness were troubling him. Below, I give what I believe is a correct summary of his interesting recital of the dramatic events he witnessed during Houston's bitter 1859 campaign for governor of Texas, which resulted in his election.

Before it skips my mind, I want to tell you about the serious, almost fatal trouble I got myself into on account of Old Pete, the General's stallion; then, I will tell you about one of the greatest political campaigns ever seen in the whole country.

My master had sold "Raven Hill" to Mrs. Sarah Goree, an old Alabama friend, and moved into Huntsville, buying his town house — the place the people now call the "Mount Vernon of Texas." It was understood that he sold his Raven Hill plantation to get ready cash with which to make his race for governor and to clear up a few debts he had made during the panic of 1857.

A little over a block from the house there was a fine spring, and about three hundred yards below it the waters from the spring made a big pool, which everybody called the "baptising pool."

One morning I put a halter on Old Pete and led him down to the pool. He was drinking out of the pool when Miss Nannie or rather Miss Nancy Elizabeth, the oldest daughter, who was thirteen, ran up to where Pete and I were standing. I do not know why I did it, for the General had often warned me that Old Pete was vicious and wouldn't stand any foolishness. The General was about the only man who could ride him.

Miss Nannie had a small switch in her hand, and I just couldn't keep from telling her to hit Old Pete. I guess

I thought I would have no trouble holding him. She struck the switch against Pete's nose, and up he reared and would have plunged after her if she had not jumped back very quickly. In doing this, she fell into the pool, which was over her head. I turned the horse loose, and jumped in the water to save her. Some of the other servants up at the spring heard the noise and ran to us and helped me save Miss Nannie from drowning.

It happened that my master was at home that morning. He and everybody else on the place rushed down to the pool. The General didn't say anything. He let his wife ask me and their daughter a great many questions. Then the General took out his long pocket knife and cut a good-sized limb from a sapling and pointed to the stable. I knew that my time had come.

He took me inside one of the barns and gave me one of the soundest thrashings a boy ever got. But, in after life, I have felt that perhaps the whipping was a great honor after all, for there are not many boys who have the distinction of being whipped by one of the great men of history!

That was the only time the General ever whipped me, and never again did he have to speak to me a single harsh word.

Just before my master started on his speaking tour, he and the mistress decided to move to their home at Independence, which was near Brenham in Washington County. The General bought three hundred head of sheep and put them out to graze in a pasture he leased from a Mr. Moore. He then turned the sheep over to his son, Sam, Jr., the eldest boy, who looked after them with the

help of a man named Jack. While we were away on the
campaign, I overheard my master say to one of his old
army cronies that the sole reason he bought the sheep was
to give his boy a chance to get some practical experience.
He even told this friend that if Sam, Jr., got swindled out
of the sheep, it might be a good thing, and teach him
business lesson No. 1, which he said was to look after
your own interest first. But, while we were gone, young
Sam, Jr., and his helper fattened the sheep, drove them to
Galveston, and sold them at a fine profit.

The 1859 race for governor and other Texas offices was
made only a little over a year before the South seceded
and organized the Confederate nation.

I went through it all, but I can not remember one-tenth
of the abuse, vilification, and false testimony directed at
my master. I had thought the first campaign was a bitter
one, but this was worse and my master's enemies more
vindictive.

All the newspapers in the state, with the exception of
one weekly in San Antonio, were untiring in their attacks
on my master. I am sure my master could have sued some
of them for libel, but it was his policy to let many things
go unanswered.

Governor Runnels and his Lieutenant-Governor, Mr.
Francis R. Lubbock, were considered two of the shrewdest
politicians in the entire country. Both of them were fearless old-fashioned Southerners, who believed in states'
rights and secession as much as the most devout man
could believe in the Bible. They had built up a powerful
political machine, made up of lawyers, politicians, plant-
ers, ranchers, and business men.

They had gone further than this — had practically organized the churches to fight the General. The slavery and states' rights questions had become such burning issues throughout the country that the word of God was not spoken as much on Sundays from the pulpits as attacks on one side or the other, according to whether the preaching was in the North or the South. But, in Texas, every circuit rider and pastor, hardly without exception, got up and denounced my master, and tried to blacken his character by saying he was a drunkard, although everybody knew he had quit his drinking and had joined the Baptist Church.

Among the favorite arguments they used against my master were that the General was an "independent" candidate, and had no party to back him up. They charged that he was a turncoat and traitor to Texas and the South, an anti-secessionist and anti-states' rights man in league with the "black Republican abolitionists" of the north, and that he had voted with the Yankees many times during the long years he was a United States senator against the interests of all Texas and all Southern people.

My! it was exciting to hear the great speeches my master made. And you only had to hear him, and see his earnestness and patriotism, to know that he meant what he said and was telling the truth. He was such an eloquent talker and expert campaigner that the other side did not dare to have their best orators meet my master in joint debate.

As my master had predicted, he won the election. But before I give you the results, I want to tell you about one of the best speeches he ever made in his life during that gubernatorial race, and all this happened over eighty years ago!

As far as I know, the only other man living today who heard the speech, which was made at Madisonville, Texas, or who ever saw General Sam Houston (besides his only living son, now eighty-five years old, Brigadier General Andrew J. Houston) is the Hon. John T. Browne. Mr. Browne is now in his ninety-fifth year, and is the oldest living ex-mayor of the city of Houston, Texas.

But back to the speech. My master had heaped many political honors on Hon. Francis R. Lubbock, the first one being in 1837 when he appointed him Comptroller of the Texas Republic. Mr. Lubbock, a fiery South Carolinian, had been a staunch supporter of the General until the secession issue arose. He had been elected as Lieutenant-Governor two years before when Governor Runnels defeated my master, and was now running for reelection as Lieutenant-Governor on the Runnels ticket.

When General Houston paused in the midst of his Madisonville address to take a drink of water, using the big gourd that hung beside the speaker's stand, a loud voice, far back in the crowd, cried:

"What about Lubbock? What about Frank Lubbock?"

Rising to his full height and looking the audience over very deliberately, the General shouted in his deep voice that might have been heard half a mile:

"Lubbock! Lubbock! That man has all the attributes of a dog save one — fidelity!"

A hushed silence, and then deafening applause followed this thrust at a political opponent.

Later, Mr. Lubbock ably served one term in 1861-1862

as "War Governor" of Texas and was then appointed
aide-de-camp by President Jefferson Davis, with whom he
was captured and imprisoned in a northern fort after the
close of the Civil War.

General Houston turned the tables upon Governor Runnels in this second race by polling 36,257 votes to 27,500
cast for Governor Runnels, thus winning the governorship
by almost the same majority Governor Runnels had received two years before.

I heard my master tell his friends several times why he
made such a hard fight for the governor's office. He said
he didn't care for the honor, as two states and a republic
had already trusted him with many offices, and that he
didn't care for the $2,000 a year salary, as he had enough
to live on comfortably.

He explained that his wife and children opposed him
running for the governorship in his old age, as for thirteen
years he had spent most of his time away from them in
Washington as United States Senator.

He said that his principal reasons for wanting to be
the Governor of Texas was his belief that Texas was
destined to become not only the Empire State of the Union
in size but the Empire State in wealth and population,
and that he believed that if any man could keep Texas
from seceding from the Union, he might be able to do so.

My master was just like a young country boy getting
ready to make his first trip to town when we began to get
things together to move to the Governor's Mansion at
Austin in the fall of 1859.

The day before we left for the State Capital, the General sent Uncle Joshua forward with two wagons filled

with the family belongings, including the piano. The next morning, we saw the big yellow coach off, driven by Tom Blue, the coachman, within the coach being Mrs. Houston, the children and two maids.

As was the General's habit when the family went visiting or traveling, he had me drive him ahead of the coach in the old top buggy. We went so fast with the black mare that within a little while we had left the coach behind and every now and then we would stop and wait for the coach to catch up with us.

At one of these stops, under the shade of a tree, the General suddenly turned his keen eyes on me and asked me to say my a-b-c's. I recited the alphabet without making a single mistake. He then had me spell many words, and was kind enough to give me easy, simple words.

Then he reached into his pocket and pulled out a newspaper and handed it to me, telling me to read a few lines here and there, and that I might skip the words I didn't know.

You cannot imagine how good I felt when my master said:

"Let's hurry on, Jeff. You will be a learned man yet."

I was very proud, even if I didn't do very well at the reading. I remember that the newspaper had an article about my master, and that its name was *Telegraph and Texas Register*, then published at Houston. That paper certainly had a heroic and romantic history, as I found later when I had at last educated myself sufficiently to enable me to read as well as most people.

The *Telegraph* was started at San Felipe de Austin in the fall of 1835, just as the Texas Revolution was getting

under way, by Mr. Joseph Baker and two brothers,
Thomas H. and Gail Borden, Jr. The paper became the
official government paper, and continued publication until
1880. In that year it was reorganized, and from the re-
organization was born one of the great Texas newspapers
— *The Houston Post*.

Mr. Gail Borden, Jr., was quite an inventor. From his
experiments with a buggy, which he rigged up with sails
to be driven by the winds over the Texas prairies, arose
the term "prairie schooner." He also invented the process
of condensing sweet milk, now known as Borden's Con-
densed Milk.[1]

I did not get to sleep one minute the first night in
Austin. The long dusty trip from Independence had caused
my mistress to have a bad attack of asthma. She was so
sick she didn't dare lie on the bed for fear she might
strangle. The General had me pick up leaves in the yard
and put them in dishpans and tin buckets all around her
chair. I kept the leaves burning all night. The smoke from
the burning leaves always did her more good than all the
medicine she ever tried.

Within a few days, after we all got settled down to
our new life in the Governor's Mansion, the General had
me drive him and Sam, Jr., over to Bastrop, thirty-five
miles away, where he was going to enter his son in Colonel
Allen's Academy. Sam, Jr., was sixteen, and was a fine,
strapping, likable boy.

We all stayed at the Nicholson Hotel. The next morning we drove over to the Academy so that the General
could tell Colonel Allen what he wanted Sam, Jr., to
study. As we came into the grounds, we saw two or

three companies of cadets drilling. Their captain was a
fine-looking man from Mississippi — Captain Joseph D.
Sayers. When Texas quit the Union, he joined the Confederate army and in a short time was a colonel. After
the Civil War, he was a congressman for years and finally
the Governor of Texas.

That night at the hotel, we met a great many people
from Austin, all of whom my master knew. District court
was in session, and on the bench was Judge A. W. Terrell, whom I have mentioned before and who wrote an
article in the Southwestern Historical Quarterly about the
General, just fifty-three years afterwards.

In this article, the Judge gave my master's ideas on
educating his son:

"He told me that he wanted his son to be well grounded
in the history and constitution of the United States, to
continue his study of English grammar, and to have daily
practice in writing until he could write well; to cypher to
the 'single rule of three', and learn how to calculate interest so as to protect himself in business, and did not wish
him to 'waste time' on Greek and Latin, nor keep him at
school for years to learn the higher branches of mathematics.

" 'For what profit,' he asked, 'is there in learning to tell
how long it will take a ray of light from some distant star
to reach our planet?'

"He wished to take Sam from school before he was
twenty years old and place him in a clerk's office, or store,
to come in contact with men and learn the 'great book
of human nature.' He said that if Sam was kept at school
until he was older in order to study Greek, Latin and

advanced mathematics he would return home 'a graduated fool.'

"It may be well doubted," concludes Judge Terrell,
"whether a university education would have better quali-
fied General Houston to lead the rugged men who drifted
to the frontier of civilization or to hold his own when sur-
rounded by the turbulent spirits so often opposed to him."[2]

The hotel was so crowded that I didn't get to sleep on
a pallet on the back porch as I usually did in our travels,
but had to sleep in the loft in the barn. But it looked like
I wasn't going to get to bed at all, for lawyers John Han-
cock, George W. Paschal, and Jack Hamilton from
Austin were attending Judge Terrell's court. After supper,
all of them crowded around the General to hear some of
his stories. They sent me and a colored boy by the name
of Joe, across the street, many times, to the saloon for
toddies, although my master kept to his bitters and orange
peel.

They all told innumerable campaign yarns and other
stories and did not break up the meeting until about one
o'clock in the morning, and after that the mosquitoes kept
me awake the rest of the night.

The next morning the General ordered his breakfast
very early, as was his custom until he got to be very old,
and we were on our way to Austin by daylight.

What is it anyhow — Fate or Providence, or just plain
luck?

Just think of it! In less than ten years after the General
had saved me from the clutches of that Simon Legree
fellow, Mr. McKell, I was the trusted right-hand servant
of the Governor of the great State of Texas. I had learned

to read and write, had plenty to eat and wear, and was sleeping on a pallet beside the door of the room in which slept one of the famous men of our country! I guess people would have to go back to the ancient days of the Romans to find rulers who had slaves for "office boys" and drivers, such as I was.

From the piney woods of East Texas I had been brought to the beautiful capital of Texas, and would see there with my own eyes some of the most exciting events that ever took place in any state capital of America.

* * * * *

"I think I've already explain'd t' you," remarked Jeff one day, "how my master made almos' as many enemies by fightin' for free educati'n of the young folks, wheth'r they wer' white or black, as he did by fightin' the secession'sts.

"In those days, many people both North and South didn't want t' be tax'd to pay for schoolin' oth'r folks childr'n. Let those who're able send their childr'n to the pay schools or else hire a home teach'r — a tuter they call'd him. An' mos' of th' slave-own'rs tho't it mighty foolish to try an' educate any of th' slave boys an' girls."

I found Jeff was almost a fanatic on the subject of universal education. He was highly "edified" to know that the Texas people are taxing themselves more heavily and spending more money on the education of the children of its colored citizens than any other state.

[48]

With a population of nearly six million in 1930, Texas contained 854,964 Negroes. Of the present scholastic population of 1,579,841, 238,966 are colored, of which number 30,482 attend high schools.

The total estimated value of the Permanent School Fund of Texas is around $100,000,000.00, consisting of high-grade securities and lands, a great deal of which is oil or prospective oil property.

From the earnings of this great fund (the principal may not be expended for any purpose) $22 is allotted each year for the education of *each child, white and black alike*. In addition, the school fund annually receives nearly forty million dollars from its share of ad valorem, gasoline, liquor, occupation, and other taxes.

All Negro public schools and colleges in Texas are State supported, and participate on a fair, pro rata basis with white schools in the apportionment of funds for free tuition and free text-books. There are several colleges for the education of Negroes, supplemented by twelve junior and senior high schools.

Jeff Hamilton in 1935 in Belton, Texas, with his ninety-fifth birthday cake presented by the Sam Houston Chapter of the Daughters of the Republic of Texas. *Courtesy of the Railroad & Pioneer Museum, Temple, Texas.*

Chapter V

"I APPEAL TO THE GREAT SOUL OF THE NATION!"

It was not long after my master had asked me to say my a-b-c's on the lonely road which led from Independence to Austin that my mistress and her mother, Mrs. Lea, and some of the older children took great interest in the efforts I was making to educate myself.

Time and time again they would correct some bad blunder I made in speaking, but always in a kind and considerate way. Several times they gave me one of the children's school-books or a child's book printed in simple words, although in those days books, newspapers, and magazines were very scarce.

I was making considerable progress in learning to read and write. What was more important, I afterwards learned, was the way in which I seemed to understand what I was studying and the knack of acquiring knowledge of things in the outside world beyond the commonplace happenings of everyday life.

One thing above all others I first learned about my master and his family, and that was their patriotism which was shown in an intense love of Texas and the United States. They were Southern to the core, Mrs. Houston being a native of Alabama, and the General a native of Virginia — both of them pure-blooded, all-Americans.

Of course, all of us knew that General Houston looked

upon the American Union with the same feeling of love as had his friend, General Andrew Jackson, who always spoke of my master as "one of my boys from Tennessee." More than once, President Jackson had said of my master —"The world will take care of Sam Houston's fame!"

"Old Hickory, Old Hickory," my master would say, "if he were living today, our ship of state might make port safely!"

Governor Houston and his lady were about as handsome and important-looking a couple as ever have received guests in the White House of Texas.

I saw the executive mansion again during the Centennial celebration of Texas independence in 1936, and it looked almost as it did eighty years before when I served my master there during the time he was governor.

I have several articles from magazines and newspapers about the mansion and one of them reads:

"Its chaste Georgian lines rank it as an outstanding example of Southern colonial architecture. One of its most distinctive features is the winding stairway in the reception hall, which is so nearly perfect that it has been inspected, described, and copied by eminent architects through many years."

We all moved into this magnificent home, with its beautiful grassy yard and fine trees, in the fall of 1859, just after the General was elected governor on his anti-secession platform. Both the governor's mansion and the State Capitol had been finished four years before, in 1855, during the term of Governor E. M. Pease, who was a Whig and had come to Texas from Connecticut. They built both of the buildings with some of the $10,000,000 the State had gotten from the United States Government in settling the boundary dispute between Texas and the government under the 1850 Compromise Law. For that amount, Texas gave to the Federal government over 100,000 square miles of its western territory. I have saved a fine copy of a drawing of the two buildings and the grounds made by an Austin man over seventy-five years ago. The capitol building burned down in 1881. A deal was soon made with moneyed men in Chicago and England who built a $3,500,000 capitol building in 1888, which was the biggest in the world, and for which Texas gave them 3,000,000 acres of ranch land in the Panhandle. It was a fine trade all around. That land is now settled up with farmers and cattle-growers and is supposed to be worth over sixty million dollars, but our people got a great capitol for little or nothing, as when the trade was made, the land was probably worth only a few cents an acre.[2]

When we moved from Independence to Austin, the baby of the mansion was Andrew Jackson Houston, then five years old, but now eighty-five. When my master or the mistress had nothing special for me to do, I used to play stick-horses with the little boy. Today, he looks very much like his father looked, is about the same size and has his ways of acting and talking, but he wasn't the king of the place long, as in August, 1860, the last baby of the eight children, Temple Lea Houston, was born.

"Little Andy," as young Andrew Jackson Houston was called, achieved state-wide fame shortly before the birth of Temple Lea by subduing the State Senate which was unfriendly to his father's legislative program and his views on secession. The boy was one of the most likable children I ever knew, but he was also one of the most mischievous.

He was a great favorite with Major E. W. Cave, the Secretary of State, whose office was next door to that of the General. Often, he would visit the Major, who would usually place him at a big desk and give him plenty of paper, pencils, and goose-quill pens so he might write his official "letters" and draw all kinds of "pictures" of soldiers and other scenes.

One windy March morning, young Andrew Jackson reached his "office" about eleven o'clock and asked Major Cave for writing material. The Major must have been in a bad humor that morning or else he was interrupted at his busiest time, as he answered the boy so sharply that the little fellow's feelings were wounded.

Leaving the office in a fit of temper, Andrew Jackson climbed the stairway which led to the Senate chamber on the second floor of the capitol, where that august body was in session. Finding the sergeant-at-arms away from his post beside the door and seeing the massive key hanging in the lock, the son of the Governor locked the door of the Senate and made away with the key. Running as fast as he could to the Governor's Mansion, he threw the key into the tall grass by the walk.

The dignified Senators did not learn they were locked up until shortly after adjournment at noon. The sergeant-at-arms, aided by Senators, spent an hour trying to find another key and then looked everywhere for a rope or ladder with which to escape from the hall.

At first, the hungry lawmakers took the matter in a

good natured way, thinking that some member was playing a practical joke. But it was not long before they began to suspicion that some Houston man had turned the key upon them.

At last, the angry Senators had to open the high windows and call for help. Quite a crowd soon collected along the walks beneath the Senate chamber. Everybody except the Senators were enjoying the show, and making all kinds of suggestions at the expense of the "prisoners." I remember that one man, seeing Senator Bob Taylor at the window, who was a stickler for the Constitution, yelled at him:

"Hey! there, Taylor, we've got you constitutional pie-eaters where we want you now!"

Meantime, someone told my master that he had seen his son fooling with the lock of the door. The General sent me flying to the Mansion for Andrew. "Little Andy" left his kite-flying and slowly came to his father's office. Under threats of a whipping and a long term in jail, the boy finally told where he had thrown the key. He had kept the Senators behind locked doors for over two hours!

I remember how the General used to laugh about this incident. He told one friend that his six-year-old son had shown more generalship in handling the members of the Legislature than he himself had shown with all his power as Governor.

No one will ever know how proud I was when my master told me, "Jeff, I hereby promote you to work for me as my office boy."

I really held down three jobs at once, as I was still his house-boy and drove his buggy for him. I may not have

[55]

fully appreciated the confidence and the responsibility of my new place, nor understood what a chance it gave me to hear interesting things and see many important people. The General was well-known all over the United States and in foreign countries because he had defeated and captured Santa Anna at San Jacinto and had been twice the President of the Texas Republic and for thirteen years United States senator. He was known all over the world on account of getting Texas recognized as a Nation and getting her admitted into the Union as a State. Hardly a day passed that some old Texas friend or some famous man from some other state or country didn't visit him. He was so hospitable he always asked all of them he liked to eat at the Mansion, if he could find a place for them at the table, and to stay all night, if there was a bed left.

There were two men in whom I believe the General had more confidence and liked more than any other of his friends. They were Major E. W. Cave of Houston, his Secretary of State, and Dr. Ashbel Smith, who lived on the Bay east of Houston near Cedar Point, the General's summer home.

Dr. Smith was a rich man and a bachelor. He came to Texas from Connecticut just after the battle of San Jacinto, and my master liked him so much that he appointed him surgeon-general of the army right away. When the fight started on annexing Texas as a state, the General appointed the Doctor Minister to England and France, and President Anson Jones, who followed the General and was the last President of Texas, did the same thing.[8]

I shall never forget one afternoon in the Governor's

office when the General and several of his friends were talking over old times. Dr. Smith or Major Cave — I don't remember which — asked him in a joking way how many men he had killed in duels. You see, my master was about the first big public man in the United States and Texas who had the bravery to refuse to fight under the foolish *code duello.*

It required high moral courage to do this, and most men didn't have back-bone like my master to face the public and the jeers when they refused to meet a man who had challenged them. His enemy would then "post" his name in a signed statement, stuck up on trees and houses where everybody could see it, which said that the man challenged was an infamous chicken-hearted coward, or something to that effect. When Texas became a state in 1846, and the first legislature met, an anti-duelling law was passed which outlawed the whole thing in Texas.

The General told his friends he had fought but one duel, and was sorry that he fought that one. He said that when he was congressman in Tennessee, Major William White became very angry about some post office appointment, and challenged him to shoot it out. The General said he went to his old friend and patron saint, General Andrew Jackson, and borrowed two of his duelling pistols, as Old Hickory was a famous duellist. He spent several days with him at the Hermitage, practicing with the pistols, and getting suggestions from the General. The duel was fought across the state line in Kentucky, and while Major White was badly wounded, he got well.[4]

One time about a dozen of these challenges had piled up in my master's office when another one was received.

The General threw the letter over in the pile with the other challenges, and said to his secretary:

"Write this irate gentleman that he'll have to wait his turn!"

Dr. Smith then said the General didn't need pistols in a duel, that all he needed was a good hickory stick such as he used on William Stanbery, Ohio representative in Congress. There was one man in the crowd who hadn't heard about it. The Doctor explained that Congressman Stanbery was against President Jackson and his friends and was a lobbyist for some Indian agents appointed by a former administration. The General came to Washington from Arkansas, where he was living as a chief with the Cherokees, to expose these agents. Mr. Stanbery in the House and in the newspapers said the General acted crooked himself in trying to get government contracts to supply the Indians with goods, and that the President and his Secretary of State were in the crooked deal, too.

About supper-time one night the General met Congressman Stanbery on Pennsylvania Avenue and the Congressman stuck his pistol against the General's heart, but it snapped. The General then nearly beat Mr. Stanbery to death with his walking cane. He was laid up for days.

Mr. Stanbery then brought charges of contempt against my master in Congress. The trial lasted over a month, and he was convicted, as Congress was against President Jackson. That didn't satisfy Mr. Stanbery, so he filed criminal charges against my master. That trial lasted a long time, and the General was defended by a lawyer named Francis Scott Key, author of "The Star Spangled

Banner." My master was fined $500, which President Jackson cancelled.[5]

A funny thing happened about all this many years after my master died. I was working for a man by the name of Stanbery, who raised chickens in a big way on Walnut Creek in Williamson County. I got to thinking about the name one day and found out that this Stanbery was a nephew of the one my master whipped with the hickory cane.

When my master was elected Governor of Texas, he tried in every way he could until war broke out to pour oil on the troubled waters. He told the Legislature in his first message little or nothing about the slavery trouble, but wanted them to act at once with him to get the children better public schools, straightening out the State finances, and giving protection against the Indians to people living on the frontier.

The campaign of 1860 for president was the most exciting political race we have ever had in our country, I am sure. I had always been in the habit of looking closely at everything, and my master had also taught me to observe everything. I am certain that I saved him from being shot and it came about in this way:

I had noticed for several days two young men by the names of Lafayette Cook and ....Montgomery hanging around the capitol building late in the evening. They were ring-leaders in a secret political club or society known as the Knights of the Golden Circle.

Once or twice I caught them peeking into the window of the Governor's office. I hid in the shadow of the corner of the building, when I saw them coming up the walk the third time. Cook stole up to the window and pulled out his pistol and aimed it at my master. Montgomery asked him why he didn't pull the trigger. Cook said that if he fired his gun he was sure to hit Mr. Penland, the General's secretary, whose desk was between them and the General. I rushed in and told Mr. Penland what I had seen and heard. He hurried out of the capitol in his shirt sleeves, overtook the two men, and said:

"Gentlemen, is there anything you want? We've noticed you peering through our office window. If there is anything you desire, come into the office like men and we'll treat you right. But if you hang around here like you have been doing, there is going to be plenty of trouble!"

Mr. Penland told the General what had happened, and advised him to arm himself and to be very careful in going from his office to the Mansion. My master said:

"Penland, I am not afraid of any man that ever lived, and it would not look right for a governor of a state to go around with a big pistol buckled to his side."

In those days, most men carried their six-shooters in a holster strapped to their leather belts. Mr. Penland told my master that his life was more important than the dignity of the office of Governor, and suggested that the General buy a pair of derringers. The General asked how he might conceal the derringers, if he got them, and what a pair of these pistols cost.

"That's easy," answered Mr. Penland. "Just simply have two pockets made in the back of your pants and call them 'hip-pockets.' The derringers only cost $30 a pair."

After breakfast the next morning the General had me

hitch up the horse to the buggy, and take him with two
pairs of pants to the Burleson House, where a German
tailor had a shop. The General explained what he wanted,
and the tailor promised the pants for the following day.
I then drove the General to the post office and to Han-
cock's store, where he chatted with friends, and from there
to his office in the Capitol. He gave Mr. Penland a
check for $30, telling him to cash it in the Treasury De-
partment, but my master was such a fearless man he
didn't bother to carry the little derringers for more than a
month or so.

I remember a great deal about the last political speech
my master made in Austin, which was in September,
1860, shortly before the election of President Lincoln.
This big Union mass meeting, held in the interest of the
Bell ticket, met near the Baptist Church, not far from the
Governor's office, where a speaker's platform had been
placed.

There was a lady in the crowd by the name of Mrs.
Schoolfield, who had often said that she would blow
General Houston's head off if he ever again slandered
her husband in his speeches. Major Cave, the Secretary
of State, was there making notes of the speech, and on
the platform were other Houston men, such as Judge
James M. Swisher, and Colonels A. B. Norton and A. J.
(Jack) Hamilton, a former Congressman, who was appointed Governor of Texas by President Johnson right
after the close of the Civil War.

In the middle of his speech, the General said:

"Schoolfield is another black sheep in the flock; he's
so 'wishy-washy' he won't stay in the flock, and he won't

[61]

stay out of it. He's bleating behind another black sheep —
'Wiggletail' — (my master meant U. S. Senator Wigfall
from Texas) and 'Dirty Shirt Bill' Scurry, who hasn't
bathed in a year, is running behind both of them, bleating
against the Union and me!"

Mrs. Schoolfield jumped up, flourished a big horse-
pistol, and shouted to the General and dared him to "say
it again," stating that if the General repeated what he
had just said that she would blow his brains out.

My master laughed, the crowd roared, and Colonel
Hamilton hollered to the General to repeat what he had
said.

The General paid no attention to the angry lady, but
repeated what he had said and added many other telling
blows. Then he said that Senator Douglas was also running around the country, bleating like the rest of the black
sheep. He said that Senator Douglas didn't care whether
slavery was voted in or voted out, if the people would
only be silly enough to vote Douglas into the president's
chair.

It always happened that when some old friend went
back on my master, he was in for an awful licking by my
master on the stump or in a letter. So, in his speech, my
master paid his compliments to General William R.
Scurry in a most amusing way. It brought so much applause the General couldn't go ahead with his speech for
several minutes.

Until the secession trouble started, General Scurry had
been a strong Houston man. He was a very able and
eloquent lawyer, and came from a fine family, but was
very careless about the way he dressed and shaved. I've

seen him when he looked almost like a tramp. I will read you what the General said:

"That man Scurry has also been going around with the rest of the black sheep, vilifying his old friend Houston. Professor Shumard, our State Geologist, came to me the other day and wanted me to appoint him as State Geologist for two years more. I told him that I would do it on one condition, and that was that he would show me that he was a real geologist by making a detailed report to me on the composition he found on 'Dirty Shirt Bill' Scurry's neck. I have his scientific report, and it shows that he has found six distinct strata of filth on Bill Scurry's neck, and in the lower strata, next to the hide, he has discovered the fossil remains of animalculae!"[6]

The General caused the greatest enthusiasm by that speech. He surprised everyone by his eloquence, as my master had got up from a sick bed to speak against the advice of his wife and doctor. I have since then read his speech many times, and I want you to quote some of his closing remarks:

"I appeal to the nation . . . I would appeal rather to the great soul of the nation than to the passions of a section . . . I ask not the defeat of sectionalism by sectionalism, but by nationality . . . If, through division in the ranks opposed to Mr. Lincoln [the General was a Bell man] he should be elected, we have no excuse for dissolving the Union. The Union is worth more than Mr. Lincoln, and if the battle is to be fought for the Constitution, let us fight it in the Union and for the sake of the Union. Let the people say to these abolition agitators of the North, and the disunion agitators of the South, 'You

[63]

cannot dissolve this Union. We will put you both down; but we will not let the Union go!' "[7]

My master had been called an infamous traitor by the states' rights men, who said that if Mr. Lincoln, the "Black Republican" candidate, should be elected, *it would be the same as a declaration of war against the South, and would mean secession!*

Sometime before the election was held, my master and most of the well-posted men felt confident that Mr. Lincoln would be elected President, and if he was elected they almost knew that the South would secede at once. My master still hoped, in spite of all this, that he could save Texas for the Union. And at our next meeting I will relate what I think is the grandest chapter in the General's whole life.

* * * * *

The "irrepressible conflict" seemed necessary to fuse into a nation the loosely-knit states of the American Union, which were much like a group of republics.

In his neutral and enlightening book, "The Story of the Confederacy," Robert Selph Henry, Southern historian, states:

"The Confederacy was a belated attempt to exercise the right to withdraw from the United States of America... bound to be a conflict so long as the nation existed 'half slave and half free,' especially so long as no man knew whether, at last, his final allegiance was due to his state or to the Federal Union of States... One of the tragedies of the War between the States while it lasted and for many years afterward, was that neither side could realize nor appreciate for what the other was fighting. To many of the North, the war of the South was a wicked and causeless rebellion undertaken to keep black men and women in slavery; to the like-minded in the South, the war of the North was a design of conquest and subjugation, hypocritically masking itself as a crusade for freedom."

As Sam Houston had predicted, Senator Douglas' Kansas-Nebraska Bill nullified Clay's famous "Compromise" acts, and divided the nation into two hostile camps —slavery and anti-slavery. The Dred Scott decision of 1857, the Lincoln-Douglas debates of 1858, and, late in 1859, John Brown's raid and execution—all combined to arouse fierce hatreds and passions.

Unfortunately, the pulpit, press, and political opportunists North and South excited the public mind into a state of crusading frenzy. The South viewed John Brown as a justly hung felon, while the North placed upon his head a martyr's crown.

In 1860, leading newspapers, followed by enthusiastic mass-meetings, urged General Houston to run for the presidency as an independent candidate in the belief that his statesmanship and experience might unite the country and avert war among the states. His fellow-veterans in a "convention" on San Jacinto battlefield, adopted resolutions recommending General Houston "to the nation as the people's candidate for the presidency."

In the *New York Herald* morning edition of Wednesday, May 30, 1860, nearly all of the front page is devoted to an account of a mass meeting held at Union Square,

New York City, on the evening of May 29, 1860, which is quoted in part as follows:

THE PRESIDENTIAL CAMPAIGN.

The Sam Houston Demonstration at Union Square.

Ratification of the Texan Nomination.

General Sam Houston Put Forth as the People's Candidate.

THE BATTLE GROUND OF SAN JACINTO.

Speeches of Ex-Mayor Mickle, Clinton Roosevelt, Dr. Stephen Hasbrouck, Fenelon Hasbrouck, D. D. Atchison, J. W. Harris and A. W. Bryce.

SONGS FOR THE CAMPAIGN,
&c., &c., &c.

The vicinity of Union Square, from the locality of the equestrian statue of Washington to several hundred feet beyond, was the scene of considerable noise and excitement last evening, in consequence of the friends of Gen. Sam Houston assembling there in large numbers, publicly to respond to his nomination for the Presidency, made by the people of Texas on the "battle ground of San Jacinto."

The following is the notice that drew the multitude together:—

THE PEOPLE'S CANDIDATE FOR PRESIDENT.
GENERAL SAM HOUSTON.

The citizens of New York, without distinction of party, are invited to meet around the statue of Washington.

[66]

"I Appeal to the Great Soul of the Nation"

From about six o'clock in the afternoon a few stragglers were to be seen gathering about the park in Union Square, and endeavoring to secure eligible positions beneath the shadow of Washington's statue. As the evening wore on to the hour appointed for the opening of the meeting, the crowd increased in density, and the wide space from Fourth Avenue to Broadway, and all around and about the square, was jammed up with the miscellaneous and apparently highly delighted multitude. The windows of the neighboring houses and hotels were filled with ladies and gentlemen, who looked on in calm serenity, no doubt believing, with the poet, that "distance lends enchantment to the view." The platform was erected immediately beneath the statue of Washington, and, as this was in the immediate path of the various cars and omnibuses, it was not surprising that the dense mass of people every moment grew larger. Added to these very attractive features, there was very excellent music discoursed during the evening by Shelton's brass band, while occasional rockets were fired and cannons discharged. A large number of boys were also employed to march in procession about the platform with lighted flambeaux, which added something of an imposing character to the scene. At the head of the platform was a portrait of General Houston, looking extremely warlike, with the following inscription:

> **FOR PRESIDENT**
> ## GEN. SAM HOUSTON
> He follows right and goes where justice leads.
> An honest man no party platform needs;

There were a number of inscriptions, all favorable to the hero of San Jacinto....

Then followed a detailed account of the meeting, including excerpts from the speeches of many prominent citizens, among whom was Clinton Roosevelt, grand uncle of our present president. Mention was made of a large number of campaign songs and one, "San Jacinto Campaign Song No. 1, Houston and the People," was given in full. Sam Houston's letter accepting the San Jacinto nomination, dated May 17, 1860, was also quoted in its entirety.

The Democratic party was hopelessly split into three factions, resulting in the nomination of three distinct Democratic tickets, headed respectively by Stephen O. Douglas of Illinois, John C. Breckenridge of Kentucky, and John Bell of Tennessee.

In the convention held at Baltimore by the faction which styled itself the "Constitutional Union Party," on the first ballot Sam Houston received 57 and Senator Bell 58½ votes for nomination as president. One of "Old Sam's" supporters was Clinton Roosevelt, grand uncle of our present president. General Houston withdrew his name, after the first ballot, since a "whispering" campaign in the convention attempted to bring to life ghosts of his marital troubles while governor of Tennessee and his life among the Cherokees after he resigned the governorship.

The Republicans nominated Abraham Lincoln — lanky rail-splitter and story-teller — while back in Texas, Governor Sam Houston tried valiantly to stem the incoming tide of Texas secession. — L. H.

Chapter VI

"I REFUSE TO TAKE THE CONFEDERATE OATH!"

At last, the day came upon which Mr. Lincoln was elected our president.

For some months I had noticed that my master was aging fast. At times he would walk with a crutch, and used his cane all the time now. But his eyes were clear, and his mind as keen and sharp as ever. He was almost sixty-eight early in 1860. His old wounds, which I had dressed hundreds of times, were paining him more than usual, especially during the cold, damp winter months.

Early on the morning of election day, I drove my master down to the polls. I sat in the buggy in front of the Calhoun House, where the election was being held. It was raining like everything. Before the General went in to put his ballot in the box, he stood awhile under the balcony of the hotel and talked to some friends. I was not over two or three feet from them, and in spite of the rain could hear everything they said.

I heard the General say that slavery was a damnable thing at best, and that he didn't believe in human slavery nor in secession or disunion either. He said he hoped God in some way might perform a miracle as of old and save the country from destruction. There was the greatest excitement ever seen in this country over the election for

president. The General went in to vote and within less
than five minutes he came out and ordered me to drive
him to his office in the State Capitol.

When we got to his office, Mr. Penland, the General's
secretary, asked him if he had voted yet. When the General told him he had just voted, I could tell from the way
Mr. Penland talked and acted that he was dying from
curiosity to know exactly how the General had voted.
Anyhow, it was not long until the secretary could stand
it no longer, and simply had to ask the General how he
voted.

I could see that my master did not like the question,
as he looked at Mr. Penland in a kind of strange, dignified
sort of way. But before he could answer one way or the
other Major Cave, the Secretary of State, rushed into the
office and handed me some papers to take to town. I had
to leave the office with my own curiosity unsatisfied, and
was afraid when I got back to ask either the General or
his secretary anything about it. I believe until this day that
the General did not tell anyone how he voted. He made
speeches for Senator Bell, but said in one of them that he
didn't believe Senator Bell had a ghost of a chance. I have
always thought that the General had reasoned it out that
he ought not to throw his vote away on a losing horse like
Senator Bell, and may have voted for Mr. Lincoln, believing that he would do more than anybody else to keep
the Union together, but, outside of that point, the General
did not agree with Mr. Lincoln on many other questions.

It was on January 28th that the State Convention of
Secession met at Austin, in the capitol building. They
drew up an ordinance of secession without wasting any

time, and set February 1st as the date for the delegates to vote on it. Just before 12 o'clock noon that day, the Convention decided to ask the General to appear before it. They knew that nearly everyone of the delegates was for secession and that the General couldn't change a single vote at that late date. But they wanted to show him a courtesy on account of his long fight for Texas independence and annexation and all he had done for the State.

A committee of six members was appointed to ask my master to appear before them. The only two men I knew on the committee were Mr. William Montgomery, a Baptist preacher, and Colonel William P. Rogers, who was a distant cousin of the General and who had fought with him in the Creek Wars under General Jackson.

The General accepted the invitation, and I hurried to bring him his coat and hat, also giving him his comb and brush to tidy up his hair. But he did not wear his hat. I followed my master and the committee up the stairs, but they hurried into the House of Representatives, and some one slammed the door in my face. But I had made up my mind nothing would keep me from the room. I ran up the stairway that opened into the balcony, and managed to get in without anyone seeing me. I crawled behind one of the posts where I could see and hear everything but where I could not be seen from the floor of the house.

There were many of my master's close personal and former political friends there who were members of the Convention and who had joined the secession movement.

The General was given the seat of honor beside Judge Oran M. Roberts, who was called the "Old Alcalde" and who was then chief justice of the supreme court.

My master rose to speak. You could have heard a pin
drop. I can remember only a few of the things he said,
but I best remember how he said them and how he acted.
He began by saying:

"All of you know that I am opposed to secession, and
all of you know my convictions on the subject. I have
taken an oath to support the Constitution of the United
States and its flag and the Constitution of Texas and its
flag. I almost died fighting for that flag, and I almost died
fighting for the Texas flag. I have served Texas under
both of those flags for a long time. Gentlemen, you cannot
forget those two flags — you cannot withdraw from the
Union.

"The country is just now in a state of prosperity. To
secede from the Union and set up another government
would cause war. I advise you to remain in the Union.
For, if you go to war with the United States, you will
never conquer her, as she has the money and the men.
If she does not whip you by guns, powder, and steel, she
will starve you to death. Now, if you go to war, it will
take the flower of the country — the young men. I know
what war is. I have been in it often and do not want any
more of it. War is no plaything and this war will be a
bloody war. There will be thousands and thousands who
march away from our homes never to come back. There
will be numberless mothers and children made widows and
orphans. I advise you to settle this matter peaceably.
Where there is union there is strength, and if you break
the Union you will wreck the whole fabric of the Constitution. No, I will never agree to sign Texas away as a
seceding State."

At this point in his speech, my master's voice choked with emotion, and tears — the biggest tears I ever saw in my life — rolled down his cheeks.

"I will show you the wounds I received in fighting for Texas and the Union you would destroy," added my master. And then my master placed his hand on his right thigh, bared his right arm, and pointed down to his ankle, and said:

"A barbed Indian arrow struck that thigh. I will take that wound to my grave. It has never healed. This arm and shoulder were shattered by Indian rifle balls. My ankle was broken to pieces at San Jacinto," he concluded and limped to his seat.

There was a deep silence, when Colonel Rogers rose and asked the General:

"Well, Sam, do you believe that your wife and daughters ought to scrub their clothes at a wash-tub and cook meals in pots over a hot fire? Before I would suffer my wife and daughter to cook and scrub, I'll wade in blood up to my neck!"

My master answered that washing and scrubbing were honorable and that no white woman had ever died from honorable work.

Then, Mr. Montgomery got up and raised a secession flag over the General's head, and asked him if he would rather give up the governor's office or join the secession plan.

My master answered:

"The reason I wanted to be governor of this state was to help it on its feet, and now everybody seems to be getting along nicely. I am not particular about the office.

I have a home and livestock and can live without the office. I feel that the Government has been paying me for past services in her hour of need rather than for present services. No, I will never give up the Constitution or the Union."

The Convention then voted to adopt the Ordinance of Secession, which carried by a vote of 174 to 7 votes. The ordinance was then submitted to a vote of the people. The election was held on February 23, 1861, and the vote was 46,129 for secession to 14,697 against secession. March 5th was the day fixed for Texas to join the Confederate nation, and March 16th the time for State officials to take the oath of office.

On the latter date, the secretary of the convention began to call the roll of State officials, so that each one of them might take the oath of allegiance which the convention had prescribed. The first name called was that of "Sam Houston." The General had stayed away on purpose, and after his name was called several times, his office was declared vacant, and Mr. Edward Clark, the lieutenant-governor, was sworn in as governor. The only other state officer who refused to take the oath was Major E. W. Cave of Houston, the General's Secretary of State. My master had ended his long public career.[1]

Between the time the first and second secession conventions met, my master made a trip to a number of the larger towns and cities in the State in a final effort to stop the secessionists. They could not stop my master from speaking at any place, although other Union speakers were driven out of town when they tried to talk. Uncle Joshua did a great deal of the driving that winter and spring.

As we came in sight of Belton (the very town where I now live!) a man riding a winded horse overtook us, waving something in his hand and shouting at the top of his voice.

As he reached the side of the buggy, he stopped and handed the General a big letter, sealed with wax.

My master got out his spectacles and opened and read the letter. With a very serious look on his face, he said sharply:

"Jeff, turn around; we must hurry back to Austin at once!"

When we got to Austin late that evening, he sent me with a message to four of his most trusted friends, having me tell them to meet him right away in the governor's office.

All of these four friends were true Union men. I built a roaring log-fire in the fire-place, and brought in a bucket of fresh water from the well just ouside the Capitol.

Without stopping to explain why he wanted to see them, my master read the letter aloud to them, and then passed it over to them, so each one could read it himself.

I heard every word of the letter the General read. It was from Mr. Abraham Lincoln, and it said that he would be president in about two weeks. He offered to make the General a major-general in the United States Army, and also to send to the Texas coast a fleet with 50,000 Federal soldiers, so that my master might put down secession in Texas.

My master then left to a vote of his friends just what he should do about the matter. One of his advisers voted to accept the offer, but three of them voted against the

[75]

proposition. The reason these three men voted against the idea, they said, was because over two-thirds of the voters of Texas had just voted for secession, and they didn't believe that even an army of half a million men could change the opinion of the Texas people, and that that kind of invasion would end with much needless slaughter. They also said that up to that time the State had not seceded from the Union in an official way.

The General took the letter, and went over to the fireplace. Throwing it into the blaze, he said:

"Gentlemen, I have asked your advice, and I will take it, but if I were ten years younger I wouldn't."[2]

The General then had me take him down to Cedar Point, his summer home on Trinity Bay across from Galveston. I remember hearing him say he had bought the place back in 1837 for $8,500. After looking after some business there, he had Captain Palmer, who ran my master's sail-boat, load the boat with salt and potatoes, and sail to Galveston.

The General had some posters printed and tacked on trees and buildings all over the town, which announced that he would speak there the next day. The secessionists tore down the posters, and threatened to hang the General if he tried to speak in Galveston. His friends came to him and begged him not to speak on account of the high feeling. But the General had made up his mind to speak, and I knew that no one could stop him. He went to the manager of the Tremont Hotel and paid him the money out of his own pocket for the right to speak on the balcony the following day.

It looked like there would be a riot when my master

came out on the balcony and began his talk. But the crowd quieted down when they saw General X. B. De-Bray, a Frenchman, who was a close personal friend of the General, surround the big crowd with a regiment of Confederate volunteers, and let it be known to everybody that if any man dared to touch my master, he would shoot him down. General DeBray also told them that while he was in favor of secession himself, he believed in fair play for both sides.

My master certainly was in fine speaking form that morning. He got a chance several times to take advantage of something that happened while he was speaking and turn it into the strongest kind of argument against what he called the "folly of secession." A horse got frightened while he was talking, and kicked himself out of his harness and almost wrecked the buggy. The General stopped a minute, and quietly said:

"Let old Dobbin alone; he is trying a little practical secession!"

About that time, the horse got tangled up in the bridle lines and stumbled to the ground. His owner began to beat him with his whip. As the horse finally got to his feet, and the teamster started to put the broken harness on him and hitch him to the buggy again, the General said:

"See how it works? You can see in what a fix he was brought back into the Union!"

The crowd couldn't help but roar with applause and laughter.[8]

Having given up the office of governor of Texas rather than to take an oath against his conscience, the General got ready to leave Austin. Within a few days, Uncle

Joshua started several wagons ahead, loaded with household goods, including barrels of glassware and ornaments, and several boxes of books and papers which the General always carried with him from place to place.

Then, Tom Blue drove the great yellow coach and its four horses up to the entrance of the Governor's Mansion. Soon, it was on its way with Mrs. Houston, the children and the colored maids. The rest of the Negroes followed in a wagon.

My master and his wife planned to visit her mother at Independence before going to Huntsville. I waited with the top buggy for the General, who was seeing some friends in the business part of town before leaving. When he came, we found a large amount of papers and other things which had been overlooked, and crammed them in the buggy and headed east.

Nobody will ever know how bad I felt about my master losing his office as governor. I felt that all of us were disgraced by the way the secessionists had practically thrown him out of the Capitol. The only consolation I had was that I knew only once before (in his race for governor in 1857) had he lost a battle in war or politics.

I felt like the end of the world had come, but my spirits began to revive when I saw the grand way my master was hiding the grief I knew he must be suffering every time he thought about his own Texas leaving the Union and his fear that the Union would be wrecked. I was old enough now to have a pretty good idea of what was causing the war which everybody knew would start any time. I could also have some idea of the terrible suffering that would come with it.

We had gone only a few blocks when the General said:

"Jeff, we have plenty of time now, since we are both out of office, so turn back and we'll drive over to see the Treaty Oak."

I had never seen or heard of any "treaty oak," so my master had to show me the way. We drove a few miles west until we came to the banks of the Colorado River and there stood the giant tree.

I was glad that the General decided to see the tree. It was an enormous live oak at least twice as large as any tree I had ever seen, more than 60 feet high, and I had seen some mighty big ones.

My master got out of the buggy, and stepped off the distance from one side of the branches of the tree to the other, and he counted 130 feet. That showed its branches shaded more than a quarter of an acre of ground!

I could see that my master wanted to be alone—wanted to think and meditate by himself. He walked around the tree two or three times, and then sat down on a long limb which a storm must have blown off the tree. I cannot remember, after all of these years, the exact words he used, but he called me over and had me sit down near him and said:

"Jeff, I want you to try to remember what I am going to tell you about this tree. The Indians have been coming here for hundreds of years. They would hold their war councils and have their war dances and other ceremonies under its shade. There's no telling how many times they smoked their peace-pipes here.

"It got to be looked on by them as a holy tree. It is said that one of the first treaties between them and the

[79]

pioneers was made under this very tree by Stephen F. Austin, the 'Father of Texas', which fixed the boundary lines between the two races.

"The Indian girls used to make a 'love-tea' out of the tender leaves of the tree, and they honestly believed that if they drank the tea with both eyes looking at the full moon then their lovers would be true to them forever. They also believed that if their tribe was at war and they drank the tea secretly, their lovers would be sure to come back home safely."

Just as we got ready to start to Independence again, my master told me that when he was President of Texas, a Mr. Audubon, a great naturalist, visited him in the little two-room frame house he lived in at Houston. He said that when Mr. Audubon heard about this king of all Texas trees, nothing would do until he had gone to look at it. My master said that when the scientist came back to Houston he told him he was sure the tree must be at least five hundred years old and that it should live hundreds of years more.

And do you know that during the Texas Centennial celebration in 1936 I got to see the Treaty Oak again, just seventy-five years after the time I stood under it with General Houston?

Colonel Paul Wakefield of Austin, who was an official of the Centennial, took me out to the tree with Governor James V. Allred, and I held the bridle of the governor's horse while they were taking pictures of us.

The General and I got back into the buggy. As I picked up the reins and looked at the great figure beside whom I sat, I knew that the end of the world wouldn't come for me as long as he lived, and that there must be some exciting days ahead for my hero and his worshipping slave!

*   *   *   *   *

Possibly no more graphic pen picture of Sam Houston in action was ever drawn than the one Jeff Hamilton paints in the above installment. He takes us with him from place to place as he drives his master on his final speech-making tour of the State just prior to the opening of hostilities in 1861. At many places secession mobs have driven anti-secession speakers from the platform, but cower before the courage and personality of "Old Sam."

The colored Boswell of the Hero of San Jacinto also recounts hitherto unrecorded happenings he claims took place before the Texas Secession Convention, by which Governor Houston is finally deposed from his office.

Jeff fails, however, to tell the sequel of Lincoln's offer to aid Governor Houston with Federal troops in his fight against the secession movement. Within two weeks after this offer was made, General David E. Twiggs, a Louisianian, in command of the Department of Texas, "surrenders" to Confederate leaders 2,500 Union soldiers. The Confederates take possession of all Texas forts, munitions, and $80,000 in cash belonging to the United States government. Almost immediately, the Secretary of

War in Washington, D. C., dismisses General Twiggs from the Union army.[4]

All Texas is saluting its *sixth* flag — the Stars and Bars! — L. H.

Chapter VII

AN OLD MAN'S DREAM OF EMPIRE

I knew that sometime before Texas seceded from our Union my master had nursed the idea in his mind, which grew into a hope or ambition, that he might be able in some way to wreck the Confederate nation and build up in its place another republic, something like Texas had been at first. This new country General Houston planned should be made up of Texas and most of the other Southern states, many of them being dissatisfied over the draft law and the way President Davis and his cabinet were running the government. He thought he could get a great portion of the western part of the United States to join him; and at one time thought he might conquer Mexico and add it to his proposed republic.

This idea grew stronger and stronger in my master's mind after the State of Texas made Mr. Edward Clark governor in his place. It was just like my master to talk openly and above-board about his ideas, and to write a great many prominent statesmen, North and South. The General knew his great popularity with the people, and believed that he would have little trouble in stopping new recruits from joining the Confederate army and inducing great numbers of the soldiers already in the war to desert their colors. Any other man would have been arrested and tried for high treason.

His wife saw what a foolish thing it was, and, with

the help of Mr. Powers, their son-in-law, who was a rich and successful business man, she succeeded in opening the eyes of my master as to the visionary character of his grandiose scheme. Later on I will tell you how some of his old political friends by their cold attitude, caused him to abandon what can now be rightly called "an old man's dream."

Just after he had given up the office of Governor of Texas, rather than swear to uphold the Confederate government, my master and his family visited Mrs. Houston's mother at Independence for a few months. This was in the Spring of 1861. When the hot weather came, the whole family went to Cedar Point, the summer home on the coast, fronting on Trinity Bay. It was a fine place to enjoy the sea breezes from off the Gulf, and for the children to swim, sail, fish, and play in the sunshine.

When Fall came, we all moved back to Huntsville and put up at Captain Sim's Hotel, as the General had sold his "town house" in Huntsville several years before. In the meantime, workmen were busy repairing a place the General had rented from its owner, Dr. Rufus W. Bailey of Austin College in Huntsville. The doctor refused to sell it to my master.

This queer-looking place got its peculiar name, the "Steamboat House," because it looked something like a river steamboat. Dr. Bailey had built it and given it to his son, Frank Bailey, soon after his marriage, but the couple never had lived in the house.

The "Steamboat" had two decks, one above and one below, with two turrets and a bridge. A broad stairway led to the second story or upper deck. The house was

located about a dozen blocks from the courthouse, across
the street from which almost ten years before the time I
mention, I had stood crying on a slave block, when my
master drove up in his buggy and saved me from Mr.
James McKell.

In the yard there were fig trees, cedars, all kinds of
Texas flowers, and crape myrtle. The only tree of any
size on the place was a fine oak. During the Texas Centennial in 1936, seventy-five years since the time I speak
of, Mr. J. E. Josey, owner of one of the big daily papers
of Texas, bought the Steamboat House, restored it to its
original state, and presented it to the people of Texas as a
shrine. It stands today near Houston's old Huntsville
home — the "Mount Vernon of Texas!"

The Civil War was being fought furiously on all fronts.
In Texas, and most southern states, no one was exempted
from the army. The Confederate government passed a
draft law, and under this law many young Indian braves
in Polk county, near where the town of Livingston now
stands, were drafted and taken to Virginia.

I shall never forget the time that their chief, whose
American name was Billie Blount, came to Huntsville
with about twenty of his men, to ask General Houston to
help him in his trouble. This tribe of Alabama Indians, a
branch of the Coushattas, was one of the oldest tribes in
the Southwest, and the State of Texas had deeded them
4,000 acres of land in 1854.

They brought several presents with them for the General and his folks. There were two or three blankets, some
beads, and little Indian dolls and small bows and arrows
for the children. Mrs. Houston never had liked for the

General to see his Indian friends, because she was a very
straight-laced Baptist and resented the fact that he had
lived with the Indians for some years as a chief and had
married one of their princesses. The General did not want
to offend his wife, and whenever any of his Indian friends
came to see him, to keep peace in the family, he would
usually meet them down at the big spring.

He was glad to see Chief Blount, and told him to kill
all the beeves he wanted for food, and to camp in the
pasture near the big spring that had gotten me into all
kinds of trouble with Old Pete, the stallion, several years
before, as I have already related.

I went down to the spring with my master, and he sat
there for hours with Chief Blount, just like the Indians
always did. They wouldn't say a word for a long time;
and, then, all at once, they would begin talking in the
Indian language, which I couldn't understand, and then
in the American language. The General didn't care to
smoke very much, but he took the long Peace Pipe from
the chief and pretended to smoke just to make the dis-
tressed Indian feel at home, I suppose. I heard him call
him "my brother" and "my friend."

At last, Chief Billie Blount told my master why he had
come to see him. He said that the Great White Father
must be dead, as there was so much fighting among brothers and sisters. He said his people had nothing to do with
this fighting, and that his people had tried to live peaceably
among the white people, and hadn't started any war, and
didn't think that it was right for one side in the fight to
come and put his men in the army. He said they had
nothing to fight for, as it wasn't their war, and he wanted

the General to get his men out of the army and let them come home.

My master sat with the Chief a long time, thinking over what he had told him, and at last said:

"Billie, the Confederate government has no right to draft your men in their army. It is a war between the states of the Union, and your people had nothing to do with it. I will see what I can do about it."

My master then told me to run up to the house and get him some writing paper, a pen, and the ink. When I got to the house, I found there was no ink except some we had made ourselves. You see it was not long after the Federal gunboats had blockaded Galveston and other ports when the supply of ink and many other articles made in the north gave out. But our Texas people were used to pioneering and used home-made ink. This we made out of the purple berries of the pokeweed and from blue indigo roots. We made pretty good coffee, too, from parched corn, acorns, etc., and pins and needles out of thistles and fish-bones.

I took the big pot of ink to the General with some foolscap paper, and two or three of his quill pens. These were not the ordinary goose-quill pens. The General always made his own pens by taking his pen-knife and sharpening the quills of an eagle. The eagle feathers were strong and stiff and one could write with them as well as with the finest steel pen of later times. Even a casual observer would be impressed by my master's wonderful signature written with one of his eagle feather pens.

My master wrote a long letter to the War Department in Richmond, Virginia, explaining all about the trouble of

Chief Blount and his men. He insisted that the Chief and his party stay with him for several days but they said that they were going to ride all night to get back home in time for a great tribal dance and harvest festival which began the next night while the moon was still full.

After much talking, during which time my master and Chief Blount said "good-bye" a dozen times, the Chief got on his pony. He then asked the General if he couldn't have back one of the blankets he had given him and Mrs. Houston as presents. So, the General had me to go to the mistress with a note, and she gave me the blankets and other trinkets the Chief had brought. This is a good example of what people mean when they say "Indian giver."[1]

In about nine or ten weeks, my master got an official-looking letter from the Confederate War Department which said General Lee had discharged the Texas Indians from the army and sent them home. The General made a copy of the letter, and then sent it on to Chief Blount. It was not long until two of Billie Blount's young braves rode up to the house, and gave my master a letter of thanks from the Chief, in which he said he and his whole tribe never would forget the great thing the General had done for his people, and that all of them were now happy again!

My master always had a world of friends in the city of Houston, which was named for him. In the elections, he usually got a big majority there. Houston was a town of about 7,000 people in 1863, the year in which my master died. Early in the year, his friends kept writing him, asking him to come and see them and make a speech.

I took my master to Houston in his buggy. We got there
the day before he was to make his speech, which was the
last one he ever made.[2] When we got to White Oak
Bayou, on the edge of town, a Confederate soldier stood
in the middle of the road and stopped us, asking for our
passes, saying that the town of Houston was under martial
law. My master got out of the buggy, and went up to the
soldier and looked down on him, as he was a little fellow
at least two feet shorter than the General. With majestic
bearing like he used to show when he was younger, he
spoke to the sentry in his deep voice:

"Go to San Jacinto, and there learn my right to travel
in Texas!"[3]

The soldier stood aside and let us pass without saying
another word.

When we had driven about a mile further toward the
city, we came to a long curve in the road. At this place,
the road seemed to have been built on a high ridge or kind
of embankment. We both heard a distant rumbling noise,
and my master said:

"Jeff, we'll wait here and see the iron horse go by."

I kept looking up and down the road, but I couldn't
see any kind of horse coming from either direction. But
the noise grew louder and louder. Then, two or three very
shrill blasts almost deafened me, and all at once I saw
rushing around the bend a long, black and red monster of
some sort. From its front end it was belching smoke, and
a bell was ringing from its top. The very ground under us
shook and trembled. I was so terrified that I let the reins
drop from my hands and would have jumped out of the
buggy and run away had not the General caught me by

the arm and held me in the seat. He then laughed and explained to me that I had seen a train of freight cars drawn by a steam locomotive.

People today may laugh at this incident, as they are accustomed to see all of these modern marvels without much wonder. But when I saw a train and railroad track for the first time in my life, I was not the only man, white or colored, who had grown to manhood in Texas without ever having seen such a thing. In fact, the great majority of the 600,000 people who lived in Texas during the early '60s (and 180,000 of these were slaves) had never cast their eyes on anything that might travel faster than an ox-wagon or buggy. Up to the time the Civil War broke out, there had been built in all Texas only about 392 miles of railway track, as compared to about 25,000 miles today.

Mr. E. W. Cave, who was Secretary of State when the General was Governor and who had also refused to take the Confederate oath, had, however, joined the Confederate army and was a major. He was at home on a furlough and had written my master to ask him to stay at his home whenever he came to Houston. That night, Judge A. W. Terrell, who had become a Confederate colonel, was also a guest at the major's house.

After supper, my master tried to "feel out" these two friends on the subject of stopping additional recruits from going to the front in Virginia and other states. But these two men threw so much cold water on the whole idea that my master quickly changed the subject, and did not even mention the matter in his speech the next day.

All three of the men had a big laugh, before going to

bed, at the expense of Sam Houston, Jr., the General's oldest son, who had joined the Confederate ranks. My master told them he never had tried to persuade young Sam not to fight for the South — that he was "free, white and twenty-one!" He further said that it was perfectly natural for his son to join the Confederacy, and fight for its flag, as all of his boy and girl friends were loyal Southerners, and that his father and mother were also intensely loyal to the South itself, if not to its new government.

My master then told them that one day Sam came to ask him about some matter, and that he noticed that the boy was wearing on the lapel of his coat a beautiful cluster of ribbons, which represented the Confederate colors. The General asked him what he was wearing on his coat. Sam answered that it was a "rosette," and wanted to know if his father thought he was wearing it in the right place.

"Sam," answered the General, "it would be more appropriate if you wore that rosette pinned on the inside of your coat-tail!"[4]

The next day my master made a talk that was filled with emotion and patriotism. He said that he was approaching "the narrow isthmus" which divided him from the sea of eternity beyond. Much to the surprise of his listeners, he spoke very hopefully of the success of the Confederacy, which then looked so certain after the many victories won by General Lee and Stonewall Jackson. There was no bitterness in his talk. He seemed at last to have forgiven his enemies. It sounded more like an oration made at the close of some school or college. He mentioned some of the good that the war had accomplished.

[91]

The only thing I can remember was his statement that every one was now appreciating the luxuries they had to do without and saw how little they could really live on, if they had to live simply.

During his talk a man who appeared to be about half-drunk interrupted my master by crying out "Hurrah for Jeff Davis! Down with the damn Yanks!" The General stopped a moment, and then said:

"My friend, I do not approve of cussing your worst enemy, if you can find some sensible argument to use against him. I have personally known Mr. Davis for many years. I first met him when he was a member of Congress from Mississippi, later when he was Secretary of War under President Pierce, and when he was a United States Senator while I was in the Senate. He was a distinguished colonel in the United States army during the War with Mexico, and was badly wounded near Buena Vista. He is a gentleman imbued with all the instincts of Southern honor and chivalry, but I want to tell you something you may not know about him:

" 'Jeff Davis is as ambitious as Lucifer and as cold as a lizard!' "[5]

The General wound up his speech by saying:

"Well, I made and saved Texas; and if she would be *unmade*, it should be her work — not mine!"

Before we went back home to Huntsville, my master had me drive him down to the San Jacinto battle-field, which was only eighteen miles from Houston on Buffalo Bayou. They have given the bayou a fancy name now — the "Houston Ship Channel." At San Jacinto, my master had won his greatest victory, when he whipped Santa

Anna's army of invasion, and captured General Santa Anna — who called himself the "Napoleon of the West."

The General didn't speak a word on the way — he was wrapped up in his own thoughts. Nor did he say anything to me, as he usually did, when he got to the end of a trip, but painfully alighted from the buggy. We had driven up to the big oak tree where Santa Anna had stood as a prisoner before General Houston.

The General sat on the ground under the tree for a long time, never speaking to me or looking at me. He had a far-off look in his eyes, which I couldn't help but notice were wet. It was now dark. My master knew how scared I was of ghosts and grave-yards, and finally smiled at me, and nearly frightened me to death when he said:

"Jeff, twenty-seven years ago I lay wounded for many days and nights under this very tree. There were hundreds of dead Mexicans all around me; and I always noticed that about midnight the ghosts of every one of those dead men jumped right out of the corpses and ran straight toward me, yelling at the top of their voices!"

*   *   *   *   *

My master talked to several of his friends on his return home from Houston about his "new nation." However, his health was rapidly failing and his death was not many months away, so it was not long until he must have decided that it was useless to try to disorganize the Confederate rule, although his stand caused much anxiety to his family and to Southern leaders.

Thus ended "an old man's dream of empire."

[93]

The idea of founding a great western empire first took shape in Sam Houston's mind soon after he resigned as governor of Tennessee, in 1829, and joined his boyhood friends, the Cherokees, encamped on the Arkansas.

Seeking forgetfulness in drink and the solitude of the forest, the "Raven" felt surging through his befuddled mind vague but persistent dreams of conquest.

An Indian chieftain himself, Houston believed that with his redskinned blood-brothers as allies and a force of adventuresome American riflemen, he might easily conquer Texas, and, perhaps, all of Mexico and Western America to the Pacific. The daring coup never was undertaken because of the promise exacted from Houston by "Old Hickory," President Andrew Jackson, his friend and hero.[6]

And now, the last great honor bestowed upon him by the people of Texas, over thirty years after his self-imposed exile among the Indians, had turned to ashes. A secession convention had met on the very soil he had consecrated with his blood, and had deposed him as governor because he was against secession.

Until his death, Houston maintained that he still was the governor of the Lone Star State and that his displacement was illegal.

The old warrior-statesman dreamed then of a second and a greater Texas Republic. Through clever strategy and propaganda, he would deter new Texas recruits from entering the Confederate ranks and bring about the desertion of those already in the army.

With Texas as a nucleus, he would issue one of his

stirring proclamations and enlist in his cause all dissatisfied elements of the South.'

So great had become Houston's renown for statecraft and military prowess that Confederate leaders in Richmond and in Austin did not view the matter lightly. In asking for more Confederate troops, Edward Clark, who succeeded Houston as Texas Governor, wrote President Davis:

"It is more than probable that an effort will be made soon by the submission party of the State, [Union sympathizers] with General Houston at its head, to convert Texas into an independent Republic . . ."⁸— L. H.

Jeff Hamilton on the morning of his 100th birthday, April 16, 1940, at the home of his daughter Mrs. Lina Graves in Belton, Texas.

Chapter *VIII*

SHILOH SHADOWS

I now want to tell about Tom Blue, my master's coachman, and his strange and dramatic escape to the free
country of Mexico.

Blue was one of the most remarkable colored men I
ever knew. If he could have had the same sort of chances
in youth that most white boys have he would probably
have developed into a great promoter of some kind and
made a fortune.

Tom Blue was a tall, fine-looking mulatto. He was
friendly and plausible. My master bought him on a trip
to Washington nearly twenty years before he bought me
when I was being auctioned off on the slave-block.

Blue was born in the West Indies. His former owners
certainly must have been what we used to call "quality
folks," as he had a good education and his manners were
like those of a high-class gentleman.

For several years Blue helped Esau, my master's other
servant, in entertaining the crowds of famous people who
came to see him when he was the Texas president and
later United States Senator. After the General's marriage
in 1840 to Miss Margaret Lea of Alabama, he bought
the big yellow family coach and four fine horses, and, as
Blue had been trained to ride and drive, he made him his
coachman.

This is the way Blue managed his escape:

President Abraham Lincoln issued his first Emancipation Proclamation in September, 1862. When the news reached us in Huntsville, Blue figured it out that this proclamation made him a free man, although under the laws of Texas and the Confederate nation he was still a slave.

Blue knew that Mexico, which my master called a republic in name only, did not allow slavery under its laws. He also knew that many slaves had managed to get to Mexico just like they had managed to reach Canada over "underground railways" with the help of Northern people who sympathized with us.

Blue then laid his plans carefully. He made a close friend of another slave named Walter Hume, the young son of Uncle Strother Hume, who ran Colonel Hume's blacksmith shop at Huntsville.

They ran away one Saturday night, and none of us missed them until late Sunday morning. By that time they were many miles away, and as there were no telephones or telegraph lines, no one ever tried to catch them.

The two fugitive men took no chances. They did their traveling at night and slept in out-of-the-way places during the day time.

Walter Hume wasn't a very smart Negro boy, and while they were on the way to the border, Blue won his complete confidence, and showed him a sure and safe way to get across the Rio Grande River into Mexico. He explained to Hume that the only trouble they would have would be with the immigration officers at Eagle Pass. He then suggested that since he himself spoke English as well as anyone, was well-dressed, and his skin so nearly white that he looked like a Spaniard, he could pass himself off as Hume's white owner.

Hume was a full-blooded African, and the plan sounded reasonable to him. So, every day they practiced just like actors in a theatre would rehearse their parts. Hume addressed Tom Blue as "master," and learned well to act the part of Blue's "slave."

All the officials and the people generally in Eagle Pass accepted the two as master and servant.

Blue had plenty of sense and knew that it would take some ready money if he lived in Mexico like a "white gentleman." On the day he crossed the bridge into Mexico, he sold his "slave" Hume at the bargain price of $800 cash — about one-third his market value.

The General and the Missus laughed over the escape, for reasons I will tell in a minute.

Blue lived in Mexico for several years after the end of the war. Then he came back to Texas and lived in Houston until he died. In his last days, he had become a dignified-looking old man, with a long white beard. He made a poor sort of living by stopping strangers and begging a few pennies for telling them his experiences as "General Houston's coachman," and by selling post-cards upon which were printed his picture and a short history of his life. He got some of the book stores to sell the post-cards for him.[1]

The trusting "slave" Hume had to wait almost three years for his freedom. In the meantime, his owner worked him almost to death. It was not until June 19, 1865, the year of the surrender, that General Gordon Granger of

the United States army issued a proclamation freeing all
the Negro slaves in Texas. So, you see, the 19th day of
June is the day the colored people in Texas celebrate as
their "fourth of July." Everybody in Texas, both white
and black, call the day the "Juneteenth," just as one
says the "Fourth."

But Tom Blue and his "slave" went to all their trouble
to escape just about ten days too soon. One morning
shortly after their disappearance, the General sent word
to all of his slaves to come to the front of the house after
breakfast.

My master was freshly shaved and had on his "Sunday
suit." Mrs. Houston, with several of the children, stood
beside him on the porch.

Taking a newspaper out of his pocket and wiping off
his spectacles with his handkerchief, the General said:

"I want each one of you to listen very carefully to what
I read you."

He then read every word of President Lincoln's proclamation of September 23, 1862, announcing that all slaves
in the seceding states would be declared free on the first
day of the following January.

The General then said that he didn't have to wait until
January to give his slaves their liberty — that the laws of
Texas, the Confederacy, the United States, and the higher
law of God Almighty gave him the right to free them
whenever he wanted to, and that he was glad to be able
to do it.

"You, and each of you, are now free," he said. "I know
I am your friend, and I know you are my friends. I'll

always be ready to help you when I can." His voice filled
with emotion as he concluded by saying:

"If you want to stay here and work for me, I will pay
you good wages as long as I can."

There was a deep silence for a minute, and it would be
hard for me to describe the faces of the slaves as we looked
at our master and his family, and then looked at each
other. It was one of the most solemn moments I have
ever seen. My mistress and the older children were crying;
my master was almost crying himself; and I know that
there was not a dry eye among us slaves.

At last, Uncle Joshua, who was a kind of boss and
leader among us, with a big gulp in his throat, told the
General that he was going right on working for him like
he always had done. All but one or two of the other
slaves said the same thing.

But old Aunt Liza, who was very excitable and who
was a great "shouter" at our camp-meetings, when she
"got religion," in some way got the notion that the law or
the government was going to send soldiers to take us away
from the Houston family, and began to moan and sway
from side to side. Then she took from the arms of the
nurse Temple Lea Houston, the two-year-old baby, and
hugging him to her bosom, cried out:

"Oh, Marster! O my Missus Nancy Lea! I don't want
no 'mancipation. I'se happy wid you all an' de chillun.
I ain't gwine ter be 'mancipated. Glory ter God! Halle-
lujah!"

Aunt Liza was getting very old, and all of us knew her
tragic yet romantic history.

When four years old, she and another little Negro girl

were playing by a road in Alabama when slave-thieves
came up in a covered wagon, and asked the children "to
take a ride" with them. Some months after the kidnapping,
Mr. Temple Lea, father of Mrs. Houston's mother, was
visiting in Mobile. He took his little daughter, Nancy Lea,
then four years old also, on a drive across the city. As they
were passing the square where slaves were being sold,
Nancy Lea saw the bright-eyed little Liza standing on the
slave-block, and asked her father to buy her for a play-
mate. And so, Aunt Liza had grown up with Mrs. Houston's mother, had helped raise Mrs. Houston and her
sisters and then Mrs. Houston's own children, becoming
the most loved slave in the Houston household.[2]

During the last year of his life, the General seems to
have changed his views greatly on the secession of Texas.
In one of his last speeches, he stated that he was for the
Union if it could be held together by peaceful means, but
was for the South "when the issue was made of resistance
or submission to Federal coercion."

My master could not bring himself to the point where
he might fight with his whole heart against his own people
— his own Texas.

I told before about Sam Houston, Jr., going to Allen's
Academy at Bastrop, Texas, at the age of sixteen, where
he received a good general education and military training.
At no time did the General try to bring any undue influence against his son's natural and patriotic desire to join
the Confederate army, in company with his own boyhood
friends and other native Texans.

It's hard for me to say which of their children my master
and mistress loved most. But both of them had a very deep

affection for Sam, Jr., the eldest child. He was such a fine-looking, manly young fellow, six feet in height. It must have wounded my master's pride for his son to become a private in the Confederate army and march away with a musket to fight against the very principles that his father had opposed so long and so bitterly as United States Senator and Governor of Texas.

Mrs. Houston, the mother, was heart-broken. As I have said before, she was a very religious lady. She hated war and bloodshed, as she was what would be called today a "pacifist."

Early in 1862, a large force of soldiers was camped on Galveston Island to get their final training before going East. I drove my master down to Galveston about the middle of March, so he could see Sam, Jr., before he left Texas. When the General reached the big camp, Colonel Moore insisted that he review and drill his regiment of 1100 men, among whom was young Sam. My master was as excited as a school-boy on circus day, and was "all dressed up" for the occasion. He wore the same clothes and sword that he had worn at the Battle of San Jacinto in 1836. His "uniform" was a pair of frayed-out, snuff-colored pants, a fur cap and high military boots, which looked much the worse for wear. He had on an old black coat and vest, with a United States army sabre hanging from his waist, tied on by buckskin thongs.

The General put his men through all kinds of maneuvers and after the drilling, which took place just before supper-time, nothing would do but that the "distinguished hero of San Jacinto" stay and eat with "the boys." Sam's captain, Dr. Ashbel Smith, brought Sam over to the tent where his father was camped. With young Sam was his mess-mate, Sam Jones, the son of Dr. Anson Jones, the last president of the Texas Republic. The General, the Captain, and the two boys ate supper together, which was served them on a long board table.

The name of Dr. Ashbel Smith was a kind of household word in Texas, as everybody knew him and loved him. He was one of the most remarkable scholars and diplomats of the nineteenth century. He came to Texas from Hartford, Connecticut, in 1837, the year after San Jacinto, on account of an unfortunate love affair. He was a rich bachelor, one of those smart blue-stocking Connecticut Yankees you read about in books. He was graduated at Yale University in the academic and medical departments. Then, he toured Europe and studied several years at some big Paris university. He spoke several languages and hobnobbed with kings and queens, the ministers, and generals all over Europe. Soon after he reached Texas, the General appointed him surgeon-general of the Texas army.

When the fight started to annex Texas to the Union, my master appointed Dr. Smith minister to France and England. President Jones later made him his Secretary of State during the long annexation negotiations, and then sent him as his minister to England and France, just before Texas was admitted to the Union as a state.

Dr. Smith at one time, so I have heard, in order to play a joke on his doctor friends, made a long speech in Latin before the Texas State Medical Society. Nobody understood what he was saying, but all of them including the doctor had a great deal of fun out of it, and every now and then they would cheer the doctor and clap their hands.

I am telling you all this, because many people today do not know what a great influence Dr. Smith had in Texas affairs. He was known everywhere as the "Sage of Evergreen" and the "Ben Franklin of Texas." He lived in great style on the bayshore below Houston, his home being called "Evergreen." Like many northern men living in the South, Dr. Smith turned Confederate, and organized Company C, Second Texas Infantry, which was called the Bayland Guards, as his land fronted on the "Bay."

But remember, on the other hand, thousands of Northern settlers in Texas went back home and joined the United States army. I read where two regiments of Northern volunteers were organized in Texas itself.[3]

Captain Smith was full of fun, and after supper told his young Negro boy, whom he had named "Buonaparte," to round up the other colored boys in camp. You see it was the custom during the Civil War for Confederate soldiers to take their slave-boys to war with them as personal servants. Buonaparte soon had about ten or fifteen boys "standing at attention" before Captain Smith.

First, the Captain had a barrel of sugar hauled out on the beach, and had each boy slave fill a big tin bucket with sugar. The boy who could eat the most sugar in five minutes was to receive a prize of one dollar.

Then, the Captain had a grand wrestling match between us, in which the winner was also to get a cash prize. But the big thing was what is called "a battle royal." This was a free-for-all, in which every fighter looked out for himself. It was not long until I was knocked down and trampled. Buonaparte proved himself a mighty fighter and must have got some of his skill from Napoleon himself, as he won the prize in the battle royal without trouble. The officers and privates, with few exceptions, made big bets on their favorites.

One of the most touching things I ever saw in my life was when the General called Sam, Jr., aside to tell him good-bye just before we started back home. He first gave him some of the usual trinkets and necessities of which mothers and sisters always think. Mrs. Houston and her daughters had sent a number of things for Sam's knapsack. And one of the articles that would play such a part in Sam's life as a soldier was the Bible his mother sent him. Then, I saw the General slip into his son's hand a small leather purse. My master had some weeks before that time bought Sam, Jr., a complete military outfit.

Sam and his company reached Shiloh Church, near Corinth, Mississippi, about April first. General Albert Sidney Johnston of Texas, who was the only full general from Texas in the Confederate army, was camped there with 40,000 soldiers.[4] He was from Kentucky and was one of the South's best commanders. My master had thought so much of his ability that he appointed General Johnston commander-in-chief of the Texas army a few months after the battle of San Jacinto. But General Felix Huston, who was a rich planter and hot-headed duellist from Mississippi, and who was the commander to be replaced, picked a quarrel with General Johnston, and in the duel that followed General Johnston was badly wounded.

General Johnston made a fierce attack on General Grant and his 33,000 men on April 6th, and drove the

Federals back twenty-three miles to Pittsburg Landing on the Tennessee River, where they were protected by land batteries and a big fleet of gun-boats.

The Texans captured a whole Union battery and 3,000 prisoners. But in the fight General Johnston was shot in the leg. He bled to death as he wouldn't let the doctors look after his wound until they had dressed the other wounded men.

The next morning, General Grant received 20,000 fresh troops from General Lew Wallace, the man who afterwards wrote "Ben Hur," and won back all the ground he had lost the day before.[5] The Second Texas Regiment was ambushed by the Third Iowa Regiment early in the battle, and both Sam, Jr., and his captain, Dr. Smith, were dangerously wounded. Young Sam was left on the field as dead, and checked off as dead on the records of Company C.[6]

Something caused the chaplain of the Iowa regiment to turn Mr. Sam's body over and look at him again. He thought he saw signs of life. By his side, he picked up a Bible, which young Sam always carried in his knapsack. It must have surely saved his life, as a Minie ball had gone almost through the book, stopping at the 70th Psalm, the great Psalm of deliverance, where it reads: "O God: thou art my help and my deliverer."

The chaplain then began turning the pages of the Bible, and on the front page he found written these words:

"Sam Houston, Jr.,
from his Mother,
March 6, 1862"

[107]

When the chaplain saw these lines, he jumped up and ran for a surgeon. He knew who Sam was, as he had known General Houston eight years before, when he was a United States senator, and at the time my master had granted him a political favor.[7]

The Union officers put Sam, Jr., in the hospital and soon nursed him back to life, and then sent him to Camp Douglas prison, near Chicago. Some time later he was exchanged for a northern prisoner held down South. This same old Bible which saved the life of my master's son can be seen today in the Sam Houston Memorial Museum at Huntsville.

I shall never forget the morning my master had ridden over to a neighbor's house a few miles away and my mistress was showing me how she wanted something planted in the flower garden. We both heard a weak voice calling, and looking over toward the fence on the side of the road we saw a tall man holding himself up by the palings, who seemed to be all skin and bones. He was on crutches.

It took Mrs. Houston and myself several moments to realize that the man was young Sam, Jr., standing before us alive! Never was a mother on this earth so happy. It looked like she would go into hysterics. And I was so happy, I just stood there with my eyes and mouth wide open, not being able to do a thing. But we managed to get Mr. Sam into the house, and put him to bed.

The best thing was that it just happened on the day we had a big pot of vegetable soup boiling on the kitchen hearth, and I ran and got the sick boy a large dish of the soup. Then, the strangest thing of all took place. I have always believed it was mind-reading or telepathy. My mistress and I looked out the window, and coming down the road at full speed was the General, his crutch swinging from his saddle.[8] I rushed out and helped the General off of the horse, and he hobbled into the house as fast as he could. He put his arms around Sam, Jr., and said in a kind of broken voice:

"Sam, all morning something seemed to tell me that you were alive and safe, and that you would come home to us!"

Sam, Jr., soon got well with the nursing we all gave him. Everybody dropped everything to look after the sick boy. At the time, we were living at Cedar Point, the home on the coast, and the sea-breezes seemed to help him a great deal. Captain Ashbel Smith was also recovering at his home on the bay, not many miles from Cedar Point.

It was not long until both of them went back to war, Sam, Jr., as a lieutenant and Dr. Smith as a colonel. And I want to tell you that there is one historical article I read once or twice every year. That is the article which Sam, Jr., wrote relating his war experiences, about twenty years after the close of the Civil War. The article is printed in the Southwestern Historical Quartely, and the title is "Shiloh Shadows."

But other shadows were creeping upon the now bent form of my great and beloved master — the evening shadows that come to every living person.

THE CAPITOL IN THE CITY OF AUSTIN

View of the State Capitol and Governor's Mansion of Texas, as they appeared to Hamilton and Houston in the 1850s and 1860s. Reproduced from a sketch drawn by William von Rosenberg in 1856, two years after the completion of the capitol building, which burned in 1881.

Chapter IX

"OLD SAM" FIGHTS HIS LAST BATTLE

I used to drive my master to Houston often, and spent many months there after his death, both during the Civil War and in the awful days of the carpetbaggers and reconstruction. My! but it was muddy there. There was little paving, except a few streets paved with wooden blocks and cobblestones. I have seen wagons bogged down on Main Street, with only the wagon-beds showing above the ground.

Houston was certainly a wild and woolly place in those days. Even now my hair stands on end when I think of some of the killings I saw and heard about there. Nearly everybody carried a six-shooter in his hip-pocket—especially at night.

The town was the big cotton and cattle market of Texas. Long "wagon-trains," as they called them, which were drawn by ten or more mule teams or yokes of oxen, hauled "King Cotton" for hundreds of miles.

The cowboys drove big herds of cattle from ranches as far away as West Texas and New Mexico. Thousands of bales of cotton and head of cattle were then shipped everywhere by Houston railroads or by boats from Galveston.

This trade brought vast sums of money to Houston, and the town was a paradise for saloon-keepers, dance-hall men, and knights of the green cloth. There were almost as many saloons as there were other business houses. Nearly every one of the saloons had a gambling-hall in full blast either in the back of the building or upstairs on the second floor. There were plenty of "music halls" or old-time variety shows. All of these places ran wide open, day and night, Sundays, holidays and election days, for 365 days in the year. The owners boasted that they had thrown the keys of their places in the bayou. Most of the saloons were on the west side of Main Street, and respectable women of the town avoided walking on the side of the street on which the drinking and gambling section was centered.

Nobody will ever know how many men were drugged, robbed, and knocked in the head, and their bodies thrown in Buffalo Bayou. The reason I happen to know so much about these places is because I roomed with a little Negro boy named "Spider." He was porter and errand boy in the gambling-hall above the old "66 Saloon," where the best known gamblers might always be seen. The stakes were high and poker and faro were the favorite games.

One night I saw a big cattleman lose his ranch to another ranchman in a poker game. The loser went out and in a short time returned with more money. Before daylight, he had won back his ranch and cattle, together with several thousand dollars. Sometimes, one or more Eastern or Northern gamblers came down with their smart city tricks to "make a killing" with the "rube cow-hands." But the Texas gamblers have always been the smartest in the world, and most of these fellows had to write back for money to buy a ticket home.

When the Houston gamblers got tired of betting on

cards or on the weather, they turned to one of the most novel gambling schemes ever heard of.

There were many killings taking place in Houston at that time and in two neighboring towns, Hempstead and Richmond. At Richmond there had been a long and bloody feud between two political factions, the Jaybirds and the Woodpeckers; and at Hempstead, feuds also had caused the death of many men. So, the gamblers had a blackboard painted, with a score-board upon it and the names of the three towns, which looked like a baseball scoreboard. They would then bet on which town would have the most daily or weekly killings. This remarkable "murder" scoreboard looked something like this:[1]

SHOOTING SCORE							
CITY	S	M	T	W	T	F	S	TOTAL
Houston . .	0	2	0	0	1	1	1	5
Richmond .	1	0	1	1	0	0	0	3
Hempstead .	0	0	1	0	0	0	3	4

But there were many very fine people living in Houston; in fact, the law-abiding element was in the majority. Every now and then, when the conditions became intolerable, the better-class citizens, joined by the ministers, would organize law and order leagues and appoint clean-up committees to enforce the law and drive the worst characters out of town. These moral crusades would improve matters, but within a few months the same old faces might be seen on the streets.

During my lifetime, I have seen great changes in people

and conditions, yet the one that strikes me most forcibly is in the matter of the age of people. When I was a young man, women forty years old and men forty-five were talked of as "old people," while today men and women of such ages are considered anything but old. The history books speak of "Old Ben Milam" and his men capturing San Antonio, and Colonel Milam was only forty-four. Why! my own master was only forty-three when he won the battle of San Jacinto, yet even then they were referring to him as "Old Sam," changing the nickname to "Samjacinto" after the victory.

Both in the year 1862 and early in 1863, I could not help but see that a great change had taken place in my master's appearance. He was seventy years old on March 2, 1863, his birthday coming on the anniversary of the signing of the Texas' Declaration of Independence in 1836. But he looked ten years older than he really was.

For some time my master had been talking about going over to Sour Lake Springs, as the hot waters there were known far and wide as a sure cure for many things. It was in Hardin county, between Houston and Beaumont, only about fifty miles from Huntsville. The doctors and the General's folks all urged him to spend a few weeks there.

Before he left, however, a delegation of his Indian friends came with a message of cheer from Chief Blount, who had heard in some way that my master was sick. There were eight young squaws and four braves in the party.

The General did not feel well enough to talk with them at the usual meeting-place down at the spring I described before. He had them sit in a circle about him on the big porch. The Indians and my master talked a long time in the Indian language. Before they started back to their homes in Polk County, my master asked them to sing his favorite Indian song. This pleased the Indians very much. They sang two or three songs for him, and wound up with the one he liked so well, which was sung in a low chant. It was a pretty song, but sad.

By 1862, United States warships had blockaded all the Texas ports, including Galveston, the main port. A good Union army was in possession of Galveston, with five gunboats, two transport ships, three schooners, and two boats they call "barks," standing guard in the bay.

But the Confederates made up their minds to free Galveston from the "Yankees," so, Major-General John B. Magruder called to Houston the best Southern officers he had west of the Mississippi for a grand land and naval attack on Galveston.

The Confederates had no gunboats, so they took three old river steamboats and turned them into "cotton-clads" to serve the same purpose as the Northern "iron-clads." They managed it in this way: They placed bales of cotton on the decks and sides of the vessels as "armor." As General Magruder only had a few real cannons, he had his men make wooden guns for the three ships, and then paint them to look like the real thing.

Then came up the question of "marines." Very few of his soldiers had ever seen the sea, but they had great spunk, and almost overnight they made sailors out of volunteers from the cavalry, infantry, and artillery.

The Texans won a great victory, the *Neptune* ramming

the *Harriet Lane*, named in honor of President Buchanan's niece, and forced her to surrender. The surprise attack could not have succeeded had not Colonel A. M. Hobby, uncle of ev-Governor W. P. Hobby, destroyed the light-house at Bolivar Point across from Galveston.[2]

Many of the Federal prisoners captured at Galveston were taken to Huntsville, the home of my master, and locked up in the State penitentiary. The penitentiary was only a short distance from our home, the "Steamboat House," so the General went over right away to see the Union prisoners.

When he found that both the officers and privates were being closely confined in convict cells like common criminals, the General was so angry that it looked for a minute like he was going to start a riot. He protested so strongly and with such unprintable words that the super-intendent of the penitentiary, who was his good friend, apologized to my master and the prisoners. He took some of them to his own home, and other Huntsville citizens had the others live with them until arrangements could be made to exchange them as prisoners of war with some captured Southern soldiers.[3]

About this time the most laughable thing in the world happened. Mrs. Nancy Lea, Mrs. Houston's mother, had always said that she would see to it that she was not buried in a pine box when she died. So, she ordered from the East a metallic coffin. In those days about the only coffins used in Texas were crude boxes made out of lumber by the local undertaker.

When the metal casket arrived, Mrs. Lea stood it up in the closet of her bedroom.

As I have before explained, things like coffee were forgotten luxuries in Texas when the Union gunboats blockaded the Texas ports a year or so after the Civil War started. But the General had so many friends in the North who knew him when he was President of the Texas Republic and United States senator, they managed to keep him supplied with coffee. Coffee was so scarce it cost $3.75 a pound at the stores.

The General had noticed that his coffee and sugar were disappearing very fast. He suspected Hannah and Mary, two young Negro slaves. One night after supper, he called us all together, and said that there must be some ghosts thieving about the place every night, and wanted us to help him find a safe place for his sugar and coffee.

He handed Hannah and Mary two sacks of coffee and sugar, and asked them to follow him. The two girls must have been guilty, for they looked scared and worried. When the General reached the closet door in Mrs. Lea's room, he said:

"I believe the safest place is right in the coffin in the closet there."

I do not believe I have ever seen such terror as I saw on the faces of Hannah and Mary. They almost dropped dead, as the saying goes. And they did drop the packages, and ran from the house screaming. After that night, my master always had enough coffee and sugar for his usual two morning cups.[4]

My master spent over a month at Sour Lake Springs. I did not drive him over there, and do not remember exactly who did. It may have been some friend, or Uncle Joshua. When he came back home, he was in worse

[117]

shape than when he had left. He had a bad cough, and his old wounds were troubling him more than ever. He had received the news of the capture of Vicksburg by Grant on the 8th of July, while he was at the springs. He was in very low spirits, and looked almost like a corpse. He told me the day he got back that he was a sick man and would not live another fifteen days.

I slept on my pallet in his sick room, but was up and down nearly all night, giving him his medicine. In the daytime, I fanned him to try to keep him cool, as it was very hot, and to keep the flys from bothering him. Mrs. Houston was also by his bedside all the time. One day when I was fanning him, I fell asleep, and the fan struck him in the face. He stirred and said:

"Margaret, you and that boy go and get some rest. There is no use in both of you breaking yourselves down."

Before I went to one of the outhouses in the yard to get some sleep, I heard him say, "My country! O my country!"

An hour or so before he died on the following day, Mrs. Houston sent one of the servants over to the penitentiary with a message to Major Carothers, one of my master's closest friends. He soon came, bringing with him a Presbyterian preacher, whose name I have forgotten, and two other friends, Judge A. B. Wiley and Colonel Hays.

Mrs. Houston and all of the children, except Sam, Jr., who was in the Confederate army, were gathered in the room. The minister wanted to know from my master how it was between him and his Maker. The General was in a stupor, but he rallied, turned over and looked the minister squarely in the face, saying: "All is well; all is well."

Then, Major Carothers asked him what he was going to do with me. My master looked at me, and told the Major that he had already freed me and his other slaves, but that he wanted Sam, Jr., to take good care of me, and that he knew Sam would do so.

It was almost sundown. Everybody was crying, and I was moaning with the rest, as I knew the best friend I had ever had or would ever have on this earth was dying. My master tried to speak again, but all he could manage to whisper was—"Margaret! Margaret! Texas! Texas!" These were the last words of my master as his great spirit winged its way out in the beyond.[5]

My master's body was soon laid out on the bed. The next day the Masons and Odd Fellows came to the "Steamboat House" in a body. After praying and reading out of their record books, they placed a white stock or tie around my master's neck, and put some of the Masonic garbs upon him.

The General was laid to rest in the cemetery across the road. I know that my master would have been pleased if he could have seen the simple slab that was put above his grave. He didn't want any great marble tombstone and he didn't need such a monument. On that plain slab were painted these words:

"General Sam Houston,
Born March 2, 1793,
Died July 26, 1863."

But Texas did not forget to place at the head of my

master's grave a magnificent, enduring monument. In 1907, Senator McDonald Meachum of Anderson, now of Houston, Texas, wrote and introduced a bill in the Texas Senate, which was passed unanimously. It provided $10,000 for the erection of a suitable monument to the memory of the General and specified that it must be made of gray Texas granite.

The State then employed the great sculptor, Pompei Coppini, of San Antonio, to design and make the statue.

The unveiling ceremonies took place on April 21, 1911, which was the seventy-fifth anniversary of the battle of San Jacinto. Never before had I seen such a gathering, as there were present over twenty thousand people.

The two great orators chosen for the occasion were Hon. William Jennings Bryan and Senator McDonald Meachum.

Senator Meachum explained that his mother was the real author of the bill and had inspired its introduction by him because her father—Brigadier-General G. J. McDonald of the Confederacy, who was born at Carthage, Tennessee—had been one of General Houston's most intimate friends in Tennessee.

The inscription at the base of the monument pleased me more than anything else, and I know that it would have pleased my master could he have seen it:

" 'The world will take care of Houston's fame.'—Andrew Jackson."

Chapter X

JEFF'S FAREWELL TO ARMS AND POLITICS

"Yessiree, I'm glad you decided to stay over another day, Mr. Hunt," were the words with which Jeff greeted me as he put on his spectacles to "censor" the manuscript I handed him. "There's some important things I forgot to tell that I hope you'll write down for me."

In my hotel room the night before, I had sat at my typewriter for hours (how reminiscent of youthful days spent as a court reporter!) transcribing Jeff's touching account of the last days of his master, General Sam Houston. I told myself that the next morning I would get Jeff's approval of the transcript, and take my leave of this interesting old man.

When I had finished the last page, I did not retire, as was my custom. Sitting there alone, in the stillness of the night, I read and re-read portions of the notes I had made, and the thought came that my work was not completed. Yes, I mused, Jeff Hamilton must have much of interest yet to tell—a sequel, as it were, to his rare reminiscences. He might wish to express a last heart's desire. Perchance, out of his rich experiences of almost a century, he might give me some final message—a dramatic, uplifting farewell to the world!

As we shall see, I was not disappointed in Jeff's relation of what might be termed a postscript to his remarkable story of Sam Houston and his times. Looking at me earnestly and from time to time stroking the back of the faithful Trip beside him, he began the final chapter in our many talks:

Right after my master died, Mrs. Houston found herself in a rented house with seven children and several servants to look after and without money of any kind. I think I told you before that my master was supposed to be worth about one hundred and fifty thousand dollars when he gave up the governor's office in 1861. But as this was tied up in land and mortgages and the war had killed business, he is said to have been worth only about seventy-five thousand dollars when he died, without any ready cash on hand.

Real money was very scarce in Texas, and Confederate bills had dropped to almost nothing in value. I remember about two years after the Civil War started, gold had risen over 50 per cent in value. A good pair of brogans that used to cost from $2.50 to $5.00 then cost $25.00, and flour, if you could find any to buy, cost from $50.00 to $100.00 a barrel. Two years later, early in 1864, $1.00 in gold was worth $22.00 in Confederate money, and the same shoes or boots cost $150.00 a pair and a barrel of flour $300.00 or more.

In fact, Confederate currency became so worthless toward the close of the war that one day a tipsy gentleman handed me a $100.00 Confederate bill, which bore two cents a day interest until peace might be declared between the North and the South, when I would have felt well paid for the errand which I ran for him had he given me ten cents.

I also remember about that time I swapped a young calf I owned for two or three pigs, and the man I traded with "threw in for good measure," he said, a $1,000.00 eight per cent Confederate bond. I have kept these two souvenirs all these years, although I have been offered a good price for them several times.

When the war ended, many people who had been rich in 1861 found themselves loaded down with hundreds of thousands of dollars in Confederate money. As they had no actual money and as there was no wall-paper to be had in Texas until long after the surrender, a few people I knew plastered their walls with Confederate bills of all denominations, which gave the rooms a very odd but most attractive appearance.

Mrs. Houston had a lot of practical sense, and she wisely gave up the "Steamboat House" and moved to the Independence home, which the General had owned for over twenty-five years. Two other advantages were that she would be near her mother and good schools for the children.

Uncle Joshua was away on one of his stage-coach repairing jobs when my master died. When he got back to Huntsville and learned that Mrs. Houston and the children had moved to Independence, he rode over there at once. As I have said before, the General always allowed his slaves to keep any money they made on outside jobs.

Uncle Joshua waited until Mrs. Houston had finished her dinner, and then came in and asked if he could talk to her alone. They went into the sitting room, and Uncle Joshua laid an old leather bag on the table before my mistress. He told her there were over $2,000.00 in gold and United States currency in the bag and that he wanted her to use every cent of it.[1]

My mistress was so overcome with the unselfish devotion which one of her slaves had shown, that she could not speak for a minute. But she handed the bag of money back to Uncle Joshua, and said:

"Uncle Joshua, it is noble of you to want to help us. You can have no idea how I appreciate your kindness, and I shall never forget it, but I cannot accept your savings. We can make out some way. And I want you to take your money and do just what I know General Houston would want you to do with it, if he were here, and that is give your own boys and girls a good education."

Uncle Joshua followed her advice, and today his son, Professor Sam W. Houston, is a leading colored educator and president of one of the State's colored colleges—Sam Houston Manual Training School at Huntsville.

It was not long after Uncle Joshua had offered to help Mrs. Houston with the money he had saved that the Legislature of Texas did a noble thing for her, which it did not have to do under the law. You see, the governor of Texas was always elected for two years and his salary was $2,000 a year. When the Secession Convention ousted my master from his office because he wouldn't swear to their oath, he still had a little over ten months to serve, so the Legislature ordered a warrant for $1,700 drawn for Mrs. Houston and sent it to her by special messenger.

I missed my master greatly. I was lonely without him, as I had come to depend upon him for almost everything. I just simply loved that great man, not alone for his kindness to me but for his goodness to everyone around him.

I knew that General Houston was my friend as well as my owner. Somehow I did not feel like I was his slave, but more as a part and parcel of his household and the place itself. Before he voluntarily freed us, I wasn't always thinking, like so many other slaves I knew, of some plan to escape or how I might manage to buy my freedom some day.

Then, in less than two years after my master's death, I lost my other great friend and the great friend of all mankind, black and white—President Abraham Lincoln. I shall never forget when I heard of his assassination. Mr. Sam, Jr., had gone to Houston on some business, and the day after Mr. Lincoln was shot, he came home with the news and a copy of the Houston newspaper telling all about it.

People gathered around Mr. Sam and his paper, but they acted more like they were at a funeral, they were so quiet and solemn-faced. Mr. Lincoln was so big in his mind and heart that all people with the same big souls grieved in the South as they did in the North. They hated his government and his plan of freeing their slaves, but they could not hate the man, unless they were of a low, narrow, hating class.

I heard several men say that the South surely was to suffer now, and that the President's death was the worst thing that could have happened to Texas.

Here is a copy of the "extra" printed by the New York *Herald* on April 15, 1865. You see that it is in good condition, too. Heavy black lines are on each side of every column telling of the death of President Lincoln.

Mr. Hunt, I got this paper in a peculiar way. In 1872, I was working for a man by the name of Tom Purcell, in the cedar brakes of Burleson County. He was a northern Negro, who had come to Texas after Emancipation. He was cutting cedar trees and shipping the cedar poles or lumber to a big pencil factory somewhere in New Jersey. I think it was either the Dixon or the Eagle company.

He had brought with him a copy of the *Herald* extra, and when I got married at his house, he gave it to me as a "wedding present," knowing how much I wanted the paper and how often I had read it to him, as he couldn't read himself. That is one reason why I have kept it in such fine shape all these years.

I stayed with Mrs. Houston and Mr. Sam, Jr., for several years after my master died. I did not run off and leave them without any help, as many of the colored slaves did to their former owners. They had all treated me as well as if I had been white and a member of their family.

I did a great amount of the housework and looked after the cows, hogs, chickens, and garden.

Yellow fever was a frequent visitor to Texas in the early days, especially to towns on the coast like Houston and Galveston. They did much business with ports in Central and South America, where the fever sometimes raged for years at a time.

The 1867 epidemic was one of the worst we ever had. The great trouble was that nobody knew that the mosquito carried yellow fever, and the doctors didn't know how to treat it. None of us paid much attention to the mosquitoes, except in the hot summer months, when we slept under mosquito bars made out of netting.

Many prominent people died that year from the fever. One of them was Lieutenant Dick Dowling, the 25-year-old Irish-American who won the greatest Confederate naval victory. On September 8, 1863, in a little sand fort at Sabine Pass, with only forty-one men, he drove off General Banks with his Union fleet of six gunboats and twenty-three transports loaded with 6,000 men. He sank or captured several boats, killing sixty-eight men and capturing 200 prisoners and a big supply of guns and ammunition.

I guess my colored friends and people in the North who may read my recollections will get the idea that I was in favor of the South winning the war. That was not the case, for I knew that we slaves would never be freed unless the North did win. But when you are living with people all around you who are kind and good to you and whose sons are fighting, you can't help but get some of their enthusiasm.

It was not long until the yellow fever broke out at Independence. Nurses and doctors were so scarce that my mistress helped nurse some of her friends and neighbors. She soon contracted the disease, and died within a few days. She and the General had always wanted to be buried side by side. But the danger of spreading the fever was so great that the doctors wouldn't let them take the body to Huntsville, and ordered it buried at Independence, where it now rests.

After my mistress died, I drifted from place to place.

doing odd jobs at first. The first two men I worked for were the biggest hypocrites and the meanest men I ever knew. They were even worse than Mr. McKell, the man from whom General Houston bought me, and that is saying a great deal.

The first man I worked for was named Ross, a Baptist preacher, who was always praying and shouting and claimed to be so holy that he always carried a Bible in his pocket, but if his flock could have seen how stingy and mean he was at home with us workers and his own family, they wouldn't have listened to him preach. We actually didn't have enough to eat, and he had plenty to feed us if he had wanted to do so. He had three hands and he got us up before daylight and made us go to the muddy cow-lot in our bare feet, when it was raining and sleeting. We didn't have enough clothes to keep us warm, and he wouldn't advance us enough money to buy shoes or clothing. Many a day we had to drive four miles in the woods with ox-wagons and cut cordwood and haul it back when a Texas "norther" was blowing.

The next man, a Mr. Taylor, was just as bad. He was a deacon in some other church. He agreed to pay me $13 a month if I would stay and work for six months until the crops were "laid by." I worked hard for five months, and couldn't get even a dime from him to buy tobacco.

One day I walked to Independence, which was ten miles away, and told some of my white friends of my troubles. They took me over to Judge Campbell's office. He was a big lawyer, having just come to Texas from Tennessee, where he was Chief Justice of the Supreme Court. He said that his father had known my master back there. He got in his buggy, and took me back to Mr. Taylor's place. Mr. Taylor was a very old man, and whined before the Judge, and claimed that I was a poor farm hand and that he hadn't agreed to pay me anything until I had worked for six months. The Judge said:

"Taylor, you infamous scoundrel, I wouldn't sue a man like you, it ain't worth wasting my time and court costs on a fellow like you who would try to cheat a good little Negro like Jeff, whom Sam Houston loved. And if you don't pay Jeff every dime you owe him right now, I'll horse-whip the hide off of you!"

Mr. Taylor didn't have any money, but his son was a fine young man and he told the Judge that he would pay me the money within a few weeks, just as soon as he came of age. And the boy kept his promise.

A quarter of a century passed from the day Mr. James McKell separated me from my mother, "Aunt Big Kittie," and sold me to pay his whiskey bills and soon afterward sold the rest of my family, one by one, causing them to be scattered all over South Texas, when, almost by accident, I located my mammy, "Aunt Big Kittie." She had become a very old woman, and was living about six miles from Groveton, the county seat of Trinity County.

Our joy at meeting again knew no bounds, for I had been my mother's favorite child, and I believe that I loved her more than the other children did. We sat up and talked all night. She got out an old Bible, which she said that her mistress, Mrs. Bettie Gibson, gave her before we left Kentucky. In it, she showed me the date of my birth, April 16, 1840. From her, I also learned for the first time that my father was a man by the name of Abner Hamilton, who was a large land owner in Kentucky.

In January, 1889, I moved to Belton, Texas, and have lived here ever since. For fourteen years, until 1903, I worked as the janitor of the Baylor College, which is one of the most widely known female universities in the country.

[The writer of these recollections will bear witness to the fact that the faculty and student-body view Jeff almost as an institution. His daughter's home is within a few blocks of the school. Many are the letters and little remembrances he receives from them. During home-coming weeks, when alumni renew their faith in the ideals of their alma mater, many of them come to see this interesting man, who so well expresses and so staunchly defends the principles of Texanism and Americanism!]

I have conversed with General Houston in my slumber many times, continued Jeff, true to the mysticism of his race. The first time I met him in my sleep was in 1886. It appeared to me that I entered one of the most beautiful cities I had ever seen in my life. My old master spoke to me:

"My boy, you have come to this wonderful city. Everybody is the same here. Everyone is free and kind and loving to each other. Come to the sisters and let them lead you around this great city and show you everything."

There were all kinds of flowers and shrubs lining the walks, which were made of white marble. The sisters explained everything to me. One of them raised a lid from the walk, and asked me to look down below and tell her what I saw. I looked down and told her that I could see nothing but trees and land, and stock and people. She said that that was where I had come from, and that no one was allowed to enter the city who was not chosen. Just as my master returned and started to speak to me again, the vision vanished and I woke up.

Jeff showed me a number of pictures taken of him in recent years. The first one was a very fine group picture, showing a delegation of the Daughters of the Texas Revolution, who spent the day with Jeff on his ninety-fifth birthday. The birthday cake had ninety-five candles upon it. Jeff told me that about 10 o'clock in the morning, one of the ladies asked him to give them his life's history, from boyhood. Jeff began to talk, he said, and when he had gotten to the thirty-fifth year of his life, he noticed that it was 1 o'clock and most of his visitors were snoring!

During the Texas Centennial celebration in 1936, Jeff visited the Centennial at Dallas, being the special guest of Temple Houston Morrow, a business executive and a grandson of General Houston. He was also an honored guest at other points, notably at Houston and Austin, the State Capital, where he was the guest of Hon. James V. Allred, Texas Governor, and Col. Paul L. Wakefield, widely know newspaperman and secretary of The Texas World Fair Commission.

On my last interview with Jeff, I sat with him on the long porch of his daughter's attractive home perched upon a plateau overlooking the beautiful little city of Belton. The green grass which covers the front yard sweeps down in waves from the hilltop to the street below. Just above the tops of the two majestic oaks which stand as sentinels before the house, I could see the reflection of the sinking

[131]

sun. Trip, the constant companion of old Jeff, was challenging, with his barks, a big, red rooster which had dared venture upon the lawn.

As the evening shadows lengthened, a vagrant breeze wafted to my feet a leaf from the taller of the two great oaks. It was bronzed with autumn color and provoked a thought: Here at my side was another bronzed and falling leaf, one of the few still left on the mighty tree of Texas history that had witnessed the stirring scenes of the glorious drama of the '50s and the tragic days of the '60s.

And now the sun was setting, symbolically, it seemed to me, as I looked upon the patriarchal figure at my side and realized that soon the same sun would set forever upon the long and eventful life of Jeff Hamilton.

Jeff was placidly but reluctantly smoking one of the cigars I had given him. It was a gesture of courtesy, for he loves his old pipe best of all.

As I prepared to leave, I asked Jeff to tell me just what his heart's great desire is in his old days, and if he would not give me some message to the people of Texas, something that above all other things he might like both his white and colored friends to remember. An air of wistfulness seemed to steal over his features. Perhaps, it was a longing for the presence of his master, whose absence he had felt so keenly through the years. After some moments of reflection, Jeff said:

"Almost since the day that General Houston bought me, my ambition—my life-long hope—has been that when I died I might be buried at the feet of my master. I have written to his only living child, General Andrew J. Houston, and to my master's two grandsons, Mr. Franklin Williams and Mr. Temple H. Morrow, all of whom I knew when they were babies, asking them to see if this could be done; and I want you also to help me.

"And I do have a message I want you to tell the world for me. In 1937, the San Jacinto Centennial Association of Texas invited me to attend the ceremonies at the dedication of a market at Cedar Point, where my master lived for two years after he left the Governor's office in 1861. They asked me to make a speech there. I want to read you from one of the newspapers the way I closed my talk. What I said there is my final message to the people of Texas.

" 'Let peace and harmony prevail among all nations. Let us be honest and truthful neighbors and revere the things that are fine in life. Here beneath these shade trees where I once played with Colonel Houston, I learned many things from my master. He lived as he taught me to live, and now I am an old man. I tell you these things because, were my master back on his old stamping grounds today, he would tell you the same things!' "

1. PLACE OF DEATH

STATE OF TEXAS

COUNTY OF **Bell**

CITY OR PRECINCT NO. **Temple** — **918 E. Ave. D**
GIVE STREET AND NUMBER OR NAME OF INSTITUTION

2. FULL NAME OF DECEASED **Jeff J. Hamilton**

LENGTH OF RESIDENCE WHERE DEATH OCCURRED **54** YEARS **5** MONTHS ___ DAYS. (SOCIAL SECURITY NO. ___)

RESIDENCE OF THE DECEASED | STREET AND NO. **918 E. Ave. D** CITY **Temple** COUNTY **Bell** STATE **Texas**

PERSONAL AND STATISTICAL PARTICULARS	MEDICAL PARTICULARS
3. SEX **Male** 4. COLOR OR RACE **Negro**	17. DATE OF DEATH **Mar. 30**, 1941
5. SINGLE, MARRIED, WIDOWED OR DIVORCED (WRITE THE WORD) **Widow**	18. I HEREBY CERTIFY THAT I ATTENDED THE DECEASED FROM **3-8-** 1941 TO **3-30-** 1941
6. DATE OF BIRTH **April 16, 1840**	I LAST SAW **him** ALIVE ON **1-30-** 1941
7. AGE YEARS **100** MONTHS **11** DAYS **17** IF LESS THAN 1 DAY HOURS ___ MIN ___	THE DEATH OCCURRED ON THE DATE STATED ABOVE AT **10:37** P. M.
8A. TRADE, PROFESSION OR KIND OF WORK DONE **None**	THE PRIMARY CAUSE OF DEATH WAS: DURATION
8B. INDUSTRY OR BUSINESS IN WHICH ENGAGED **None**	**Influenza** — **22 days**
9. BIRTHPLACE (STATE OR COUNTRY) **Kentucky**	CONTRIBUTORY CAUSES WERE **Pneumonia** — **12 days**
10. NAME **Acie Hamilton**	
11. BIRTHPLACE (STATE OR COUNTRY) **No Record**	
12. MAIDEN NAME **Kittie Culvert**	
13. BIRTHPLACE (STATE OR COUNTRY) **No record**	IF NOT DUE TO DISEASE, SPECIFY WHETHER:
14. SIGNATURE **Mrs. L. L. Graves**	ACCIDENT, SUICIDE, OR HOMICIDE ___
ADDRESS **Temple,** TEXAS	DATE OF OCCURRENCE ___ PLACE OF OCCURRENCE ___
15. PLACE OF BURIAL OR REMOVAL **Belton,** TEXAS	MANNER OR MEANS ___
DATE **April 3, 1941**	IF RELATED TO OCCUPATION OF DECEASED, SPECIFY ___
16. SIGNATURE **Mrs. B. Kay Murcherson**	SIGNATURE **T. E. Dixon** M.D COR
ADDRESS **Temple,** TEXAS	ADDRESS **Temple,** TEXAS
20. FILE NUMBER **63** FILE DATE **4-2- 1941**	SIGNATURE OF LOCAL REGISTRAR **W. B. Hoyle** POSTOFFICE ADDRESS **Temple,** TEXAS

Death certificate of Jeff Hamilton, who died in 1941 shortly before his 101st birthday.

AFTERWORD

Out of ancient memories, undimmed by time and unhampered by censorship, comes Jeff Hamilton's unforgettable story of Sam Houston and his times. The simple narrative of the old ex-slave makes more understandable the personality and many-sided genius of his great master.

Unlike the orthodox historian, who is usually dependent upon second-hand evidence, this colored Boswell speaks with the authority of his own personal knowledge of the people and the era of which he tells.

If our present age lacks the constructive leadership of pioneer America, it is fortunate that Jeff has given us an intimate account of episodes in the public and private life of one of the most significant men of the nineteenth century.

Authorities generally agree that the romantic and dramatic figure of Sam Houston overshadowed most of his contemporaries. The Hero of San Jacinto belongs to no one state or section but to all of the Americas, as do Bolivar and Washington.

San Jacinto was the sixteenth decisive major battle of the world. As Charles Martel, in the year 732, turned back the Saracens in their conquest of Western Europe, so at San Jacinto, in 1836, "Old Sam" forever barred the further expansion of Latin-American civilization north of the Rio Grande. The geography of what is now the western half of the United States would be recharted. The airways were cleared for the sweep of the American eagle to the Pacific. Directly and indirectly, that triumph added more than one million square miles to the area of the United States. Dedicated to the valor of Houston and his riflemen, the San Jacinto Monument towers above the old battlefield to a height of 567 feet—the highest memorial in America.

Houston's Jacksonesque love of the Union and his heroic fight for the Union, which he knew might mean political oblivion, places him alongside Webster, whose patriotism prompted him to forego the chances of the presidency, and ranks him with Lincoln in self-effacing devotion to principle.

In the heat of congressional debate, United States Senator Houston, ever an anti-secessionist and ever opposed to sectional strife between the North and South, dramatically exclaimed:

"I wish no epitaph to be written to tell that I survived the ruin of our glorious Union!"

Two inscriptions upon the monument of gray Texas granite erected to Houston's memory above his grave in Huntsville, bespeak his place in history.

Chiseled on the back of the memorial are the lines:

"Soldier under Jackson; Boy Hero of Horseshoe Bend; Congressman from Tennessee; Governor of Tennessee; Chief of the Cherokees; Commander-in-Chief of the Texas Army; Hero of San Jacinto; Twice President of the Texas Republic; United States Senator; Governor of Texas."

On the front of the statue appear the prophetic words:
'The world will take care of Houston's Fame.'

—Andrew Jackson."

BIBLIOGRAPHY

Almanac, The Texas, A. H. Belo Corporation, Dallas, Texas. 1939.

ATKINSON, MARY JOURDAN, *The Texas Indians,* Naylor Co., San Antonio, Texas, 1935.

BASSETT, JOHN SPENCER, *A Short History of the United States,* Macmillan Co., New York, N. Y., 1891.

BRUCE, HENRY, *The Life of General Houston,* Dodd, Mead & Company, New York, N. Y., 1891.

CRANE, WILLIAM CAREY, *Life and Select Literary Remains of Sam Houston,* William G. Scarff & Co., Dallas, Texas, and J. B. Lippincott Company, Philadelphia, Pa., 1884.

GAMBRELL, HERBERT P., *Mirabeau Buonaparte Lamar,* Southwest Press, Dallas, Texas, 1934.

HENRY, ROBERT SELPH, *The Story of the Confederacy,* Bobbs-Merrill Co., Indianapolis, Indiana, 1931.

HUNT, LENOIR, *Bluebonnets and Blood,* Texas Books, Inc., Houston, Texas, 1938.

JAMES, MARQUIS, *The Raven,* The Bobbs-Merrill Company, Indianapolis, Indiana, 1929.

LUBBOCK, FRANCIS R., *Six Decades in Texas,* Ben C. Jones & Co., Austin, Texas, 1900.

Southwestern Historical Quarterly, Texas Historical Association, Austin, Texas, 1898-1940.

SMITH, DR. ASHBEL, *Reminiscences of the Texas Republic,* Historical Society of Galveston, Galveston, Texas, 1876.

WILLIAMS, ALFRED M., *Sam Houston,* Houghton Mifflin Company, Boston, Mass., 1893.

WORTHAM, LOUIS J., *A History of Texas* (5 vols.), Wortham-Molyneaux Co., Fort Worth, Texas, 1924.

In the 1930s, prominent banker W. Goodrich Jones caused a small public park in Temple, Texas, to be named the "Jefferson Hamilton Park." In 1986 the park was closed and the Hamilton name was moved to this new community center in Temple.

NOTES

Chapter II

[1]CRANE, *Life of Sam Houston.* (Contains many of Houston's important speeches).

[2]HUNT, *Bluebonnets and Blood,* 219.

Chapter III

[1]GAMBRELL, *Mirabeau Buonaparte Lamar;* HUNT, *Bluebonnets and Blood,* 229, and authorities cited, 420.

[2]HUNT, *Bluebonnets and Blood,* 137; A. W. TERRELL, *Recollections of Sam Houston,* Southwestern Historical Quarterly, XVI.

[3]WILLIAMS, *Sam Houston,* 329-31; WOOTEN, *A Comprehensive History of Texas,* 85; JAMES, *The Raven,* 385; BRUCE, *Life of General Houston,* 194.

[4]A. W. TERRELL, *Recollections of Sam Houston,* Southwestern Historical Quarterly, XVI.
[5]*Ibid.*

[6]WORTHAM, *A History of Texas,* IV, 246; HUNT, *Bluebonnets and Blood,* 269; CRANE, *Life of Sam Houston,* 402; WILLIAMS, *Sam Houston,* 306, et seq.; LUBBOCK, *Six Decades in Texas,* Chapters XII-XIII.

Chapter IV

[1]HUNT, *Bluebonnets and Blood,* 359-61; and authorities cited, 425.

[2]A. W. TERRELL, *Recollections of Sam Houston,* Southwestern Historical Quarterly, XVI; HUNT, *Bluebonnets and Blood,* 219 and authorities cited 420, for first Texas free school law; Lubbock, Chapters XIV and XV.

Chapter V

[1]Hunt, *Bluebonnets and Blood*, 265-71, and authorities, 421.
[2]*Ibid.*, 341, and authorities, 425.
[3]*Ibid.*, and other standard histories; Ashbel Smith, *Reminiscences of the Texas Revolution.*

[4]A. W. Terrell, *Recollections of Sam Houston*, Southwestern Historical Quarterly, XVI, 128.
[5]*Ibid.*, 123; Hunt, *Bluebonnets and Blood*, 138; Williams, *Sam Houston*, 45-49; James, *The Raven*, Chapter XIII.

[6]A. W. Terrell, *Recollections of Sam Houston*, Southwestern Historical Quarterly, 132.

[7]Hunt, *Bluebonnets and Blood*, 269, and authorities cited, 421.

Chapter VI

[1]Hunt, *Bluebonnets and Blood*, 270; other standard histories.

[2]Bruce, *Life of General Houston*, 206; A. W. Terrell, *Recollections of Sam Houston*, Southwestern Historical Quarterly, XVI, 135; James, *The Raven*, 410-11; Williams, *Sam Houston*, 351.

[3]Bruce, *Life of General Houston*, 203-5; Williams, *Sam Houston*, 352-5.

[4]Wortham, *A History of Texas*, IV, 340; Williams, *Sam Houston*, 350; James, *The Raven*, 408.

Chapter VII

[1]See Atkinson, *The Texas Indians*, for tribal customs, mythology, and philosophy.

[2]Williams, *Sam Houston*, 373.
[3]Bruce, *Life of General Houston*, 216.
[4]*Ibid.*, 205.
[5]*Ibid.*, 215.

[6]Hunt, *Bluebonnets and Blood*, 135-40, and authorities, 417.

[7]Williams, *Sam Houston*, 324; A. W. Terrell, *Recollections of Sam Houston*, Southwestern Historical Quarterly, 123; James, *The Raven*, 415, *et seq.*
[8]Williams, *Sam Houston*, 365.

Chapter VIII

[1]FRANKLIN WILLIAMS, grandson of General Houston, to author.
[2]*Ibid.*

[3]HUNT, *Bluebonnets and Blood*, 275.
[4]*Ibid.*, 276.

[5]BASSETT, *A Short History of the United States*, 528-9.

[6]SAM HOUSTON, JR., *Shiloh Shadows*, Southwestern Historical Quarterly, XXXIV, 329.

[7]TEMPLE H. MORROW and FRANKLIN WILLIAMS, Houston's grandsons, to author.
[8]*Ibid.*

Chapter IX

[1]Old residents of Houston, Texas, relate similar accounts concerning this weird "Score-board."

[2]HUNT, *Bluebonnets and Blood*, 279.

[3]WILLIAMS, *Sam Houston*, 373; JAMES, *The Raven*, 425.

[4]FRANKLIN WILLIAMS, grandson of General Houston, to author.

[5]BRUCE, *The Life of General Houston*, 276; JAMES, *The Raven*, 433.

Chapter X

[1]WILLIAMS, *Sam Houston*, 373; FRANKLIN WILLIAMS, grandson of General Houston, states that Jeff's account of the Joshua offer to aid Mrs. Houston tallies with the facts given him by his mother.

Portrait of Jeff Hamilton, which was hung in 1975 at the Railroad & Pioneer Museum in Temple, Texas.

PUBLISHER'S POSTSCRIPT

Despite manumission, Jeff Hamilton stayed with the Houston family until the death of Margaret Lea Houston in 1867, after which he drifted as an odd jobber. He was probably married in 1872; when his first wife died has not been discovered, but they had eleven children. In approximately 1884 he became a custodian for the Baylor Female College, and moved to Belton, Texas, in 1886 when the campus moved there from Independence, Texas. For some years at the turn of the century, he was employed as a handyman by W. Goodrich Jones, prominent banker, realtor and conservationist in Temple. Circa 1912 Jeff married widow Alice Morris in Temple, and lived in her home with her grandson, George Cockrell, who still owns the home. In the Temple city directories 1913-1927 Jeff is listed as laborer and yardman.

Alice Morris died in 1922. In 1928 at age eighty-eight, Jeff moved to the home of his daughter Lina, Mrs. Charles H. Graves, in Belton where he frequently addressed students at Mary Hardin-Baylor College. In the 1930s, W. Goodrich Jones caused a small public park at the corner of Avenues E and 14th in Temple to be named "Jefferson Hamilton Park." Hamilton died on April 3, 1941, after the publication of *My Master* in 1940 and shortly before his 101st birthday.

In the mid-1970s, as part of the Bicentennial celebrations, Hamilton's great-granddaughter spearheaded a successful effort for historical markers to be erected in his memory at his gravesite in Belton and on the campus of Mary Hardin-Baylor.

In 1986, when Hamilton Park was closed, the Hamilton name was moved to the new Jeff Hamilton Community Center at Wilson Park in Temple.

Historical marker erected to the memory of Jeff Hamilton in 1976 at the entrance to the campus of the University of Mary Hardin-Baylor in Belton, Texas.

Historical marker at the gravesite of Jeff Hamilton, East Belton Cemetery on East Sixth Street in Belton, Texas.

INDEX

Entries headed by an asterisk are possibly pseudonyms.

[145]

INDEX

Rogers, William P., 71, 73
Roosevelt, Clinton, 68
*Ross (Baptist preacher), 128
Roysten, Major Martin, 21-22
Runnels, H.R., 32, 34, 37, 40, 42-43

San Jacinto, 89, 92-93, 114, 135-36
Schoolfield, Mrs., 61-62
Scurry, William R., 62-63
Seat, Reverend, 2-3
Shumard, Professor, 63
Smith, Ashbel, 56-57, 103-05, 109

Steamboat House, 84-85, 116, 119, 123
Steiner, J.M., 33
Sublett, Bolivar, 8
Swisher, James M., 61

*Taylor (deacon), 128-29
Taylor, Bob, 55
Telegraph and Texas Register
    (Houston *Post*), 44-45

Terrell, Judge A.W., 32, 33-34, 46-47,
    90
Texas, Second Republic of, 83-84,
    93-95
Treaty Oak, The, 79-81
Twiggs, David E., 81

Wakefield, Paul, 80, 131
Wigfall, Senator, 62
Wiley, A.B., 118
Williams, Franklin, 132
Williamson, Judge O.S., 32-33